Proxy Warfare in Strategic Competition

Military Implications

STEPHEN WATTS, BRYAN FREDERICK, NATHAN CHANDLER,
MARK TOUKAN, CHRISTIAN CURRIDEN, ERIK E. MUELLER,
EDWARD GEIST, ARIANE M. TABATABAI, SARA PLANA,
BRANDON CORBIN, JEFFREY MARTINI

RAND ARROYO CENTER

For more information on this publication, visit **www.rand.org/t/RRA307-3**.

About RAND

The RAND Corporation is a research organization that develops solutions to public policy challenges to help make communities throughout the world safer and more secure, healthier and more prosperous. RAND is nonprofit, nonpartisan, and committed to the public interest. To learn more about RAND, visit www.rand.org.

Research Integrity

Our mission to help improve policy and decisionmaking through research and analysis is enabled through our core values of quality and objectivity and our unwavering commitment to the highest level of integrity and ethical behavior. To help ensure our research and analysis are rigorous, objective, and nonpartisan, we subject our research publications to a robust and exacting quality-assurance process; avoid both the appearance and reality of financial and other conflicts of interest through staff training, project screening, and a policy of mandatory disclosure; and pursue transparency in our research engagements through our commitment to the open publication of our research findings and recommendations, disclosure of the source of funding of published research, and policies to ensure intellectual independence. For more information, visit www.rand.org/about/research-integrity.

Published by the RAND Corporation, Santa Monica, Calif.
© 2023 RAND Corporation
RAND® is a registered trademark.

Library of Congress Cataloging-in-Publication Data is available for this publication.

ISBN: 978-1-9774-1052-8

Cover: Mariusz Burcz/Alamy Stock Photo.

About This Report

This report documents research and analysis conducted as part of a project entitled *State Support to Violent Non-State Actors: Assessing Risks to U.S. Overseas Contingency Operations,* sponsored by the Office of the Deputy Chief of Staff, G-3/5/7, U.S. Army. The purpose of the project was to provide insight into the determinants of state support for violent nonstate actors, assess the risks that third-party support poses to U.S. overseas contingency operations, and analyze policy options available to the United States to counter such foreign support.

This research was conducted within RAND Arroyo Center's Strategy, Doctrine, and Resources Program. RAND Arroyo Center, part of the RAND Corporation, is a federally funded research and development center (FFRDC) sponsored by the United States Army.

RAND operates under a "Federal-Wide Assurance" (FWA00003425) and complies with the *Code of Federal Regulations for the Protection of Human Subjects Under United States Law* (45 CFR 46), also known as "the Common Rule," as well as with the implementation guidance set forth in U.S. Department of Defense (DoD) Instruction 3216.02. As applicable, this compliance includes reviews and approvals by RAND's Institutional Review Board (the Human Subjects Protection Committee) and by the U.S. Army. The views of sources utilized in this study are solely their own and do not represent the official policy or position of DoD or the U.S. government.

Acknowledgments

The authors would like to thank MG Christopher P. McPadden, former Director of Strategy, Plans and Policy in the Office of the Deputy Chief of Staff, G-3/5/7, U.S. Army, for sponsoring this study. We would also like to thank Mark Calvo, COL Jason Charland, MAJ Jenny Gunderson, and MAJ Constance Quinlan for their support and helpful feedback throughout the research. Within RAND, we benefited from the comments and insights of Dave Johnson and Jennifer Kavanagh. Idean Salehyan of the University of North Texas and Shawn Cochran of RAND provided invaluable reviews that greatly improved the final document. Finally, we are grateful to LTC Scott Akerley, LTC Jason Davis, CPT Taylor Allen, SGM Paul Langley, and Chris Anderson from the Asymmetric Warfare Group for taking the time to provide us their insights.

Summary

The research reported here was completed in July 2021, followed by security review by the sponsor and the U.S. Army Office of the Chief of Public Affairs, with final sign-off in June 2022.

This report examines the military implications of *proxy wars,* which we define as wars (specifically civil wars) in which at least one local warring party receives support from an external state that could be useful for waging armed conflict, such as funding, arms, equipment, advising, training, intelligence, and/or troops. More specifically, the report addresses two questions:

- What military challenges are posed by violent nonstate actors (VNSAs) who receive military support from state sponsors?
- What are the implications for U.S. defense capabilities generally and U.S. Army capabilities specifically?

To answer these questions, we first reviewed the academic, policy, and military-professional literature on the conduct of proxy warfare to identify core challenges posed by proxy wars at the strategic and operational/tactical levels of war. We then conducted case studies of four proxy wars—the First and Second Indochina Wars, the Houthi Rebellion, and the Donbas War prior to Russia's invasion of Ukraine in 2022—to assess the degree of threat historically posed by VNSAs that gain more-sophisticated military capabilities in part through state support. In the final chapter, we consider the contemporary implications of our findings, particularly for the U.S. Army.

Research Findings

The additional capabilities that state sponsors can provide to VNSAs have important consequences for the forces that oppose them. At the tactical and operational levels of war, state support to VNSAs frequently combines much of the lethality of conventional warfare with the challenges of operating against a highly dispersed enemy that has taken advantage of complex terrain and integration among civilian populations. This combination poses a number of dilemmas for the forces combating them, including whether to mass against a lethal enemy or disperse against one that targets the population, whether to emphasize force protection (such as the widespread use of armor) or the ability to interact with the population, and whether to prioritize overwhelming firepower against a dangerous enemy or the use of discriminate fires so as not to alienate the population.

At the strategic level, the increased lethality of VNSAs complicates traditional models for responding to insurgencies and other forms of irregular warfare, while the risk of escalation forecloses potential options for responding to these challenges. First, the capabilities obtained from state sponsors can make it very difficult for even capable counterinsurgents to prevail against VNSAs. These challenges call into question the ability of the United States to rely on local actors to limit its own involvement, as was the case, for instance, in Operation Inherent Resolve. Second, the increased lethality of VNSAs makes it harder for the United States to make a long-term commitment politically acceptable by limiting the number of U.S. forces at risk. Third, state support imposes limits on the ability of the United States to escalate its campaign against VNSAs (e.g., by targeting their supply routes outside of the conflict-affected country) without running a substantial risk of drawing the VNSA's state sponsor into a more direct combat role.

This report provides evidence of the increased lethality of nonstate actors when they are supported by states. In the First Indochina War, the Chinese-supported Vietminh defeated more than 10,000 French soldiers at Dien Bien Phu using dozens of howitzers, Katyusha rocket launchers, and antiaircraft artillery. The Russian-led separatist forces (RLSF) in Ukraine used heavy weaponry to destroy a large fraction of the armored vehicles of the Armed Forces of Ukraine early after the beginning of the conflict in 2014, and sophisticated RLSF air defense capabilities essentially neutralized Ukrainian air power in the period of our case study, 2014–2020. The electronic and cyber warfare practiced by RLSF provide some indication of the level of sophistication that VNSAs today can achieve when supported by a major power. As Table S.1 illustrates, the capabilities used effectively by the VNSAs in our case studies are not unique to these cases; they have been employed by a great many other groups over the years.

TABLE S.1

Examples of State-Supported VNSA Military Capabilities

VNSA Capability	Examples
Short-range air defense	• Houthis • *Contras* • *Afghan mujahideen* • RLSF • Vietminh
Antitank guided missiles/anti-armor weapons	• RLSF • *Lebanese Hezbollah* • *Hamas* • *Iraqi Shiite militias*
Artillery	• RLSF • Vietminh
Mining	• Vietcong • *Iraqi Shiite militias* • *Zimbabwe African National Liberation Army*

NOTE: Italicized examples are not assessed in depth in this report.

To the extent that the increased lethality of state-supported VNSAs imposes the sorts of tactical, operational, and strategic dilemmas described above, the United States may find that its military is poorly prepared for contingencies involving these adversaries. State-supported VNSAs may pose a qualitatively different challenge from either the sort of high-end, conventional warfare for which the U.S. military is currently preparing or the sort of lower-end counterinsurgency that the United States believes it has already mastered.

Policy Recommendations

A project such as this one cannot provide detailed guidance on how the U.S. Department of Defense (DoD) or the Army should allocate scarce resources across the full range of possible contingencies. We can, however, suggest a number of measures that DoD and the U.S. Army in particular could undertake to maintain readiness for the sort of threats posed by state-supported VNSAs, were they to decide that the risks posed by proxy warfare were sufficient to justify at least modest investments in preparing for such contingencies.

Doctrine

The range of threats posed by state-supported VNSAs is much broader than the circumstances that gave rise to the last overhaul of doctrine in the field of irregular warfare. Doctrine should accordingly be updated, with a focus on the threats posed by hybrid actors and the requirements for partnered operations involving a small U.S. military footprint. Because threats do not remain static, the Army (and the rest of the Joint Force) will need to continue to make investments in updating their understanding of evolving threats and appropriate doctrinal responses. It is therefore vital that the Army continue to resource such entities as the Irregular Warfare Force Modernization Proponent in the Mission Command Center of Excellence at Fort Leavenworth.

Organization

The demands of combat against sophisticated, state-supported VNSAs may have implications for force structure, force design, and force mix.

First, although the current focus on readiness for high-intensity conventional combat is likely appropriate for current circumstances, it is nonetheless important for the Army and the Joint Force not to lose sight of the potential demands for the types of forces that would be needed in large numbers for a hybrid contingency. These forces would likely include special operations forces, aviation, explosive ordnance disposal, human intelligence specialists and interrogators, military police (especially law and order detachments), and so on.

Second, hybrid warfare and partnered operations can pose challenges to existing Army unit structures. Because hybrid warfare involves highly dispersed operations against capable adversaries, it may require certain capabilities, such as the integration of air and ground operations, to be pushed into lower echelons than is currently the case. In partnered operations, doctrinal units are commonly broken apart and used in nondoctrinal ways. Neither of these challenges (or potentially others) necessarily dictate changes to force design. But the Army may need to at least develop mechanisms to facilitate rapid adaptation of doctrinal units.

Finally, in the more hazardous environments common in wars against state-supported VNSAs, the United States may not be able to rely on meeting many of its support demands from contracted labor, as it has in recent operations. Because the bulk of support functions within the Army reside outside of the active component, this may have implications for force mix.

Training

Training should similarly be adapted for contingencies involving militarily sophisticated VNSAs. The requirements for combat against such adversaries are different than they are for high-end conventional militaries. Unless leaders are forced to prepare for these sorts of contingencies, especially by making them a part of capstone training events, such as Combat Training Center exercises, they risk losing familiarity with the broader spectrum of military operations. Such training will be required whether the United States is engaged in combat directly or simply advising partners on how to conduct operations.

Leader Development and Education

Given the complexity of hybrid warfare, leaders must be able to adapt quickly to a wide variety of demands. It is critical that professional military education remain broad-based, including courses focused on irregular and hybrid warfare and military operations among local populations. DoD's current focus on the competition space short of armed conflict has the potential to provide important experiences to emerging leaders. But the Army (and other services) must make such assignments career-enhancing, with opportunities for promotion out of such assignments as attractive as the opportunities available to leaders who have focused on high-intensity conventional warfare. The Security Force Assistance Brigades might serve as a litmus test for the Army's commitment to preparing for the full spectrum of operations.

Personnel

Military operations conducted among civilian populations inevitably benefit from knowledge of the local society. The Army and other services could expand the number of billets for personnel with regional expertise, such as Foreign Area Officers and some intelligence specialists. Alternatively, given resource constraints, the Army could reallocate its existing level of personnel with a focus on U.S. allies and partners that are most at risk of being targeted for proxy warfare.

Contents

Figures and Tables

Figures

Tables

CHAPTER 1

Introduction

U.S. national security guidance warns that the United States is entering a new era of "great power competition," conducted in part through proxies and surrogates.[1] Yet, despite the frequency with which warnings about proxies and surrogates are made, U.S. defense policy is overwhelmingly focused on regaining proficiency for high-intensity, conventional warfare with a peer or near-peer competitor. In many ways, this focus is entirely understandable. After two decades of fighting counterinsurgencies in Afghanistan and Iraq, the U.S. Department of Defense (DoD) is concerned with regaining conventional capabilities lost in that period. To the extent that proxies or surrogates pose threats that are both serious and qualitatively different from conventional interstate warfare, however, there is a risk that DoD will be underprepared for future contingencies that threaten important U.S. national security interests.

This report examines the military implications of *proxy wars*, which we define as civil wars in which an external state sponsor provides at least one local warring party with support from an external state that could be useful for waging armed conflict, such as funding, arms, equipment, advising, training, intelligence, and/or troops, for the purposes of accomplish-

---

[1]   White House, *National Security Strategy of the United States of America*, Washington, D.C., December 2017; U.S. Department of Defense, *Summary of the National Defense Strategy of the United States of America: Sharpening the American Military's Competitive Edge*, Washington, D.C., 2018. See also U.S. Training and Doctrine Command, *The Operational Environment and the Changing Character of Warfare*, TRADOC Pamphlet 525-92, October 7, 2019; and U.S. Training and Doctrine Command, *The U.S. Army in Multi-Domain Operations 2028*, TRADOC Pamphlet 525-3-1, December 6, 2018.

ing some strategic objective.[2] More specifically, the report addresses two questions:

- What military challenges are posed to militaries like that of the United States by violent nonstate actors (VNSAs) who receive military support from state sponsors?
- What are the implications for U.S. defense capabilities generally and U.S. Army capabilities specifically?

To answer these questions, we first reviewed the academic, policy, and military-professional literature on the conduct of proxy warfare to identify core challenges that proxy wars can pose at the strategic and operational/tactical levels of war. We then conducted case studies of four proxy wars to assess the extent to which VNSAs that gain more sophisticated military capabilities (in part through state support) can pose difficult challenges to militaries like that of the United States.

The remainder of this report proceeds as follows. Chapter 2 provides an overview of the existing literature on the subject and an overview of our research approach. The following four chapters (Chapters 3 through 6) are each dedicated to a study of one of four different conflicts: the First and Second Indochina Wars from the 1950s through the 1970s; the Houthi Rebellion in Yemen (with a particular focus on the period since 2015); and the Donbas Conflict in Ukraine from 2014 to the direct, large-scale Russian intervention in 2022. Each of these chapters examines the ways in which state support provided insurgents with capabilities they could not realisti-

---

[2] This definition is similar to those of Karl Deutsch and Andrew Mumford. Deutsch defined *proxy war* as "an international conflict between two foreign powers, fought out on the soil of a third country, disguised as a conflict over an internal issue of the country and using some of that country's manpower, resources and territory as a means of achieving preponderantly foreign goals and foreign strategies" (Karl W. Deutsch, "External Involvement in Internal War," in Harry Eckstein, ed., *Internal War: Problems and Approaches*, New York: Free Press of Glencoe, 1964). Mumford defined *proxy war* as "the indirect engagement in a conflict by third parties wishing to influence its strategic outcome" (Andrew Mumford, *Proxy Warfare*, Cambridge, UK: Polity, 2013, p. 1). We use the term *proxy wars* to refer to the conflicts themselves, while *proxy warfare* refers to the practices by which those wars are fought.

cally have gained through any other means and the tactical, operational, and strategic challenges that these insurgent capabilities posed to the militaries that fought them. Finally, Chapter 7 synthesizes the findings from the four case studies and discusses the implications of those findings for DoD, and especially U.S. Army, preparations for future contingencies.

CHAPTER 2

Overview of the Military Implications of Proxy Warfare

From the perspective of the U.S. government as a whole, proxy wars have important policy implications because, in comparison with civil wars without outside state involvement, they tend to be more intense, longer-lasting, more destabilizing, more likely to involve U.S. adversaries, and more likely to escalate into interstate war. But for defense-planning purposes, perhaps what is most important is to understand how the United States could respond militarily to proxy threats and whether military preparations for such actions would differ substantially from current DoD policy. In this chapter, we examine the existing literature on the military implications of proxy warfare in three steps. First, we discuss the closely related concept of *hybrid war* and review debates about whether "hybridity" poses qualitatively different military challenges from other types of warfare. Second, we discuss two specific tactical- and operational-level challenges that prior research and experiences suggest are posed by this type of warfare. Third, we review the strategic-level challenges posed by state support for nonstate combatants. In a final section, we summarize the review and discuss our research approach for the case studies in the next four chapters of this report.

Background: Defining the Threat and Debating Its Implications

State support for VNSAs can shape the dynamics of combat in both direct and indirect ways. Such support can directly influence the course of a conflict by providing sanctuary to VNSAs and limiting the counterinsurgents' ability to escalate a war (at least insofar as they seek to avoid a wider, inter-state war). The indirect effects, however, are perhaps equally as impor-tant and more pervasive. The greater capabilities that states can impart to VNSAs, and especially greater lethality, shape the way that both insurgents and counterinsurgents fight.

The Concept of Hybrid Warfare and Its Employment by State-Supported VNSAs

From a defense-planning perspective, in many ways it is less important to understand *who* is fighting than it is to understand *how* they fight. Tradi-tionally, warfare (or at least warfare beneath the level of nuclear war) has been divided into two broad categories: conventional and unconventional or irregular. In conventional warfare, militaries try to achieve decisive effects through massed forces. In unconventional or irregular warfare, an inferior military sacrifices mass and the prospect of achieving decisive effects (at least in the short term) for survivability, dispersing forces in complex ter-rain and among civilian populations to prevent a superior adversary from defeating it.

Because states typically have access to much greater resources than non-state actors, states have commonly adopted conventional operations and tactics, while nonstate actors have relied more heavily on irregular opera-tions and tactics. The affinity between actors and types of warfare, how-ever, is far from absolute. Some states (especially smaller ones incapable of mounting a conventional defense against much larger enemies, such as Switzerland and potentially the Baltic states) have embraced irregular war-fare, while some highly capable nonstate actors have adopted conventional approaches to fighting. The key point is that military capabilities, not the state or nonstate status of actors, are what determines the style of warfare that the warring parties adopt.[1]

---

[1] The political scientists Stathis Kalyvas and Laia Balcells have demonstrated through statistical analysis the relationship between military capabilities and modes of warfare, and they have shown how the mode of warfare adopted, in turn, shapes characteristics of civil wars such as their likely duration and outcomes. See Stathis N. Kalyvas and Laia Balcells, "International System and Technologies of Rebellion: How the End of the Cold War Shaped Internal Conflict," *American Political Science Review*, Vol. 104, No. 3,

This traditional way of conceptualizing warfare, however, has largely broken down. Former Secretary of Defense Robert Gates declared that "the old way of looking at irregular warfare as being one kind of conflict and conventional warfare as a discrete kind of warfare . . . is an outdated concept."[2] Many observers have noted the prevalence of *hybrid warfare*, in which elements of unconventional or irregular operations and tactics are combined with the high lethality of conventional weapons technology and organization.[3]

Just as states can adapt irregular or unconventional approaches to war and nonstate actors can adapt conventional approaches depending on the balance of military capabilities, hybrid warfare is not the preserve of any one type of actor. Hybrid warfare tends to emerge when one of the warring parties has substantial military capabilities but still does not possess the military capabilities necessary to face its adversaries in a symmetric, conventional fight. This is precisely the situation that often arises when state-supported VNSAs fight more-capable counterinsurgents (government forces and potentially foreign forces supporting the government).

States can provide sophisticated weaponry and other materiel on a scale that nonstate actors can rarely (if ever) obtain through channels such as illicit or black markets or their own production. States can also provide military training and assistance in organization that is difficult to acquire (at least at scale and at comparable levels of sophistication) through other

---

August 2010; and Laia Balcells and Stathis N. Kalyvas, "Does Warfare Matter? Severity, Duration, and Outcomes of Civil Wars," *Journal of Conflict Resolution*, 2014.

[2]   Cited in David Sadowski and Jeff Becker, "Beyond the 'Hybrid' Threat: Asserting the Essential Unity of Warfare," *Small Wars Journal*, 2010.

[3]   The term *hybrid warfare* is closely related to concepts such as *asymmetric warfare*, *fourth-generation warfare*, *new-generation warfare*, and so on, although there are nuances to each concept, and the terms are not necessarily used consistently by different observers. U.S. military doctrine is itself inconsistent, with *hybridity* sometimes referring to a mix of actors and sometimes referring to a mix of tactics and operations. See, for instance, Frank G. Hoffman, "Hybrid Warfare and Challenges," *Joint Force Quarterly*, Vol. 52, No. 1, 2009; Frank G. Hoffman, "'Hybrid' vs. Compound War: The Janus Choice," *Armed Forces Journal International*, October 2009; Thomas X. Hammes, *The Sling and the Stone: On War in the 21st Century*, St. Paul, Minn.: Zenith Press, 2006; and Christopher O. Bowers, "Identifying Emerging Hybrid Adversaries," *Parameters*, Spring 2012.

means, such as private military contractors (PMCs) or through the non-state actors' own experience. State sponsors can also provide direct support in sustainment and logistics, an area that limits the operations of many less-sophisticated militaries and militias.[4] Thus, although proxy warfare and hybrid warfare are not synonymous, recent debates about the military threats posed by hybrid warfare can help us understand the threats posed by state-supported VNSAs when they face more militarily capable government forces (and their foreign backers).[5]

Does Proxy Warfare Pose Unique Military Challenges?

If state-supported militants tend to operate in a manner that is neither fully conventional nor fully irregular when facing capable adversaries (such as the United States), does it matter for U.S. defense planning? Or if the United States is prepared for conventional and irregular war, should the hybrid war practiced by particularly well-supported VNSAs simply be considered a lesser-included case of one or the other (or both)?

U.S. military doctrine and concepts do not provide a definitive answer. Proxy actors and hybrid warfare appear frequently in official discussions of the current and future operating environment for U.S. military forces.[6] But U.S. doctrine and concepts offer much less discussion of how to fight

---

[4]   On the relationship between state support and hybrid capabilities, see especially David E. Johnson, *Military Capabilities for Hybrid War: Insights from the Israel Defense Forces in Lebanon and Gaza*, Santa Monica, Calif.: RAND Corporation, OP-285-A, 2010; and David E. Johnson, *Hard Fighting: Israel in Lebanon and Gaza*, Santa Monica, Calif.: RAND Corporation, MG-1085-A/AF, 2011.

[5]   Again, Kalyvas and Balcells, 2010, is relevant. Kalyvas and Balcells do not directly address the issue of hybrid warfare, instead distinguishing neatly between irregular and conventional warfare on the basis of "high" or "low" military capability levels. If we think of military capabilities and military disparities as a spectrum, however, their argument would seem to imply the potential for complex mixtures of irregular and conventional modes of warfighting for intermediate values along the spectrum.

[6]   A recent publication of the U.S. Training and Doctrine Command (TRADOC), for instance, predicted that U.S. adversaries "will adopt hybrid strategies that take advantage of a range of capabilities that deny us a conventional force-on-force fight unless the situation is advantageous to the adversary. They will use proxy forces that provide plausible deniability, yet directly allow them to not only shape the battlespace, but even achieve their objectives without risking a wider conflict. Similarly, they also may choose

these forces. While the U.S. Army's Multi-Domain Operations concept, for instance, mentions proxies and unconventional warfare at many points, its discussion of how to counter them is limited to little more than the observation that the ability to fight and win against an adversary's conventional forces will cut off proxies from vital support.[7] While this observation is no doubt true in many cases, it sidesteps the issue of what would be required to confront hybrid adversaries directly, focusing instead on more traditional concerns of conventional warfare.

The broader policy literature, including statements by leading U.S. military officials and knowledgeable observers, offers more insight into the military implications of state support for militants, but it offers little consensus about the right answers. Debates in particular focus on the viability of relying on partners for such contingencies and the military preparations necessary should the United States be required to take on a more direct military role.

Many seem to believe that the United States has already found a solution for the challenges of fighting nonstate actors: the model exemplified by Operation Inherent Resolve (OIR) in Iraq and Syria. In this model, local actors carry the brunt of the fighting, while the United States supports them with intelligence, surveillance, and reconnaissance (ISR) capabilities; stand-off weaponry (including both airpower and long-range ground fires); and a limited number of U.S. advisers cooperating closely with local partners to both provide military advice and to coordinate direct support from the United States. Representative of this perspective is a statement by General Joseph Votel, then-commander of U.S. Central Command, who argued that OIR demonstrated that the United States could achieve its strategic goals in irregular and hybrid warfare without deploying large numbers of its own troops:

> We have also learned that a modest commitment of resources, applied steadily and consistently over time, and in a predictable fashion, can assist our partners in managing change, adjusting to new threats, and

---

to work with, sponsor, or support terrorist or criminal entities to achieve a similar end" (U.S. Training and Doctrine Command, 2019, p. 7).

[7] U.S. Training and Doctrine Command, 2018, p. viii.

building their own capacity to act. This has the additional benefit of lessening our own requirements in future contingencies and building our reputation as a reliable partner. Working "by, with, and through" our allies and partners allows us to multiply the effect of relatively modest commitments to ensure this crucial and truly "central" region never again requires a mass deployment of U.S. forces.[8]

This perspective presumes, however, that OIR is representative of the full range of irregular and hybrid contingencies that the United States might face. In fact, there are at least two ways in which OIR and the fight against the Islamic State were not representative of fights against hybrid opponents, particularly those supported by major powers.

First, although the Islamic State possessed many state-like capabilities, it did not receive state support. Indeed, it galvanized the formation of a broad coalition of states that were united in seeking its defeat. The Islamic State's lack of state support placed some limits on the sophistication of its military tactics and operations; although highly capable by the standards of most insurgent groups, it possessed nowhere near the military capabilities of state-supported groups like the Vietminh. It also meant that the United States faced fewer constraints on escalating the fight against the Islamic State, in contrast with many cases of state-supported militants in which the United States limited its military responses for fear of provoking a broader interstate conflict.[9]

Second, although the United States' state-building efforts in Iraq following its 2003 invasion were disappointing, by the beginning of OIR in 2014, the government of Iraq was at least reasonably functional, and it possessed the building blocks necessary for a relatively capable military (in particular, the Counter-Terrorism Service that the United States had helped to build for the better part of a decade).[10] This situation stands in marked contrast

---

[8] Joseph L. Votel, "Terrorism and Iran: Defense Challenges in the Middle East," statement before the House Armed Services Committee on the posture of U.S. Central Command, February 27, 2018.

[9] Chapters 4 and 5 of this report provide two examples: U.S. support to the government of South Vietnam and U.S. indirect support to Ukraine.

[10] This statement is not intended to minimize the importance of the collapse of the Iraqi Security Forces in the early days of the Islamic State. That collapse nearly proved

to cases in which the United States sought to support partners in states that had collapsed entirely (as in Afghanistan in 2001 or Iraq in 2003). Prior research suggests that large numbers of U.S. forces, rather than the "by, with, and through" approach of OIR, may be necessary to achieve U.S. goals in these most challenging environments.[11]

If the United States might have to deploy substantial numbers of its own forces in a future contingency against state-supported VNSAs, there is a further debate as to what would be required of U.S. forces for them to be ready for such a challenge. On one end of the debate are those who believe that the hybrid warfare often practiced by state-supported militants largely represents a "lesser-included case" of conventional warfare. According to this perspective, if a military is competent in combined-arms operations—in particular, the ability to integrate fire and maneuver across large formations—then it should be able to defeat hybrid opponents.[12] The hybrid nature of such conflicts may require added emphasis on discrimination in targeting and a robust campaign of operations in the information environment to avoid alienating the civilian population. But such additional requirements are relatively minor and should not distract militaries from their focus on large-scale combined-arms operations.

On the other end of the debate are those who claim that the sort of warfare typically practiced by nonstate actors with advanced state support requires the United States military to prepare differently than it would for conventional operations. In *Military Review*, for instance, retired Colonel John McCuen wrote:

> We need to stop planning operationally and strategically as if we were going to be waging two separate wars, one with tanks and guns on a

---

devastating for Iraq, and it offers a sobering lesson on the sustainability of many U.S. efforts to build partner capacity. Nonetheless, the Counter-Terrorism Service quickly became the core of the counteroffensive against the Islamic State and proved to be the most effective fighting force in the country.

[11] Stephen Watts, Patrick Johnston, Jennifer Kavanagh, Sean Zeigler, Bryan Frederick, Trevor Johnston, Karl Mueller, Astrid Cevallos, Nathan Chandler, Meagan Smith, Alexander Stephenson, and Julia Thompson, *Limited Intervention: Evaluating the Effectiveness of Limited Stabilization, Limited Strike, and Containment Operations*, Santa Monica, Calif.: RAND Corporation, RR-2037-A, 2017.

[12] Johnson, 2010; Johnson, 2011.

conventional battlefield, the other with security and stabilization of the population. Symmetric and asymmetric operations are critical, interrelated parts of hybrid war, and we must change our military and political culture to perceive, plan, and execute them that way.[13]

To better disentangle these debates, we examine both the tactical- to operational-level challenges posed by state-supported militants and the strategic-level challenges they pose. Following U.S. military doctrine, we understand *strategy* as "an idea or set of ideas of the ways to employ the instruments of national power in a synchronized and integrated fashion to achieve national, multinational, and theater objectives."[14] Strategy must balance the overarching objectives of a war with the means available, given political and resource constraints. *Tactics* represent the opposite end of the spectrum of military activities, encompassing "the employment, ordered arrangement, and directed actions of forces in relation to each other," usually involving smaller-scale military units conducting actions (such as engagements or battles) over relatively short periods of time and space.[15] *Operations* represent the link between the two, the synchronization of tactical actions in campaigns to achieve strategic objectives.[16] As the next two sections will make clear, there are no clear boundary lines between these levels of war; various activities and concepts frequently straddle these categories. As a general rule, the following discussion considers challenges to be primarily strategic if they refer to a country's ability to maintain political support for a war, marshal sufficient resources to achieve political objectives, or calibrate violence so that it does not exceed the value of the issues at stake. Tactical challenges, on the other hand, are matters that are typi-

---

[13] John J. McCuen, "Hybrid Wars," *Military Review*, March–April 2008, p. 113. See also Hoffman, 2009; Bowers, 2012; and Benjamin Locks, "Bad Guys Know What Works: Asymmetric Warfare and the Third Offset," *War on the Rocks*, June 23, 2015.

[14] Joint Chiefs of Staff, *Joint Operations*, Joint Publication (JP) 3-0, October 22, 2018, p. I-12.

[15] Joint Chiefs of Staff, 2018, p. I-14. There are, of course, exceptions. Some weapons (such as the United States' strategic arsenal) can be employed over very long distances, while some battles (such as sieges) can last longer than some short wars.

[16] Joint Chiefs of Staff, 2018, p. I-13.

cally negotiated by lower-level military leaders over repeated engagements to achieve the strategic intent of national leaders.

Tactical- and Operational-Level Challenges Posed by State Support to VNSAs

Although some VNSAs can become capable fighting forces without state support, nearly all observers agree that they can greatly enhance their military capabilities through state support. Even if future militants were able to obtain advanced technology with military application on open markets, certain specialized materiel and the knowledge of how to employ certain technologies in coordinated, militarily effective operations is difficult to obtain without state support. Historically, state sponsors have been responsible for providing militants access to short-range air defense (SHORAD) technology, antitank guided missiles (ATGMs) and other forms of anti-armor weaponry, artillery, and landmines (including mines much more sophisticated than the improvised explosive devices that insurgents in Iraq were employing without state support). State sponsors have also helped many insurgent groups obtain the training necessary to operate effectively at echelons equivalent to U.S. battalions or larger. These capabilities, in turn, made these forces considerably more lethal. According to U.S. estimates, for instance, Shiite militias in Iraq operating with Iranian support were responsible for nearly one-fifth of all U.S. deaths in Operation Iraqi Freedom (OIF), despite these forces representing only a fraction of the militias that the United States fought.[17]

The increased lethality of these state-supported militants has at least two important implications. First, it makes ground operations exceedingly complex by forcing opponents to deploy in ways capable of addressing both conventional and irregular warfighting challenges. Second, it exacerbates the challenge of discriminate targeting that all combatants face in irregular warfare.

---

[17] Kyle Rempfer, "Iran Killed More U.S. Troops in Iraq than Previously Known, Pentagon Says," *Military Times*, April 4, 2019.

Complexity of Ground Operations

To the extent that highly lethal VNSAs force the U.S. military to mass its forces to defeat the VNSAs in battle and/or for force protection, the VNSAs are forcing the United States out of a posture in which it can provide wide-area security for the population, the mass or disperse dilemma common to irregular warfare but exacerbated by the capabilities of hybrid opponents.[18] Similarly, to the extent they compel U.S. forces to rely heavily on armor for force protection, they are inhibiting interactions with the noncombatant population, a critical component of population-centric approaches to irregular warfare.[19] Neither of these dilemmas is necessarily insuperable; the United States, for instance, employed a combination of armor and infantry in cities at the height of the insurgency in Iraq.[20] They do, however, add greatly to the complexity of operations and the challenges leaders will face in balancing these competing demands.

Targeting Dilemmas

To limit the risks posed by state-supported VNSAs' higher lethality, their adversaries (whether the United States itself or its local partners) are likely to rely heavily on standoff fires, as the United States has in conflicts from the Vietnam War to OIR. In doing so, however, they will face the typical challenges of targeting irregular opponents who seek cover among the civilian population. Numerous studies have suggested that indiscriminate violence fuels support for insurgents and ultimately higher levels of violence.[21]

---

[18] See McCuen, 2008, and the discussion of the Vietminh in Chapter 3 of this report.

[19] Lyall and Wilson argue that highly mechanized forces have typically fared poorly in counterinsurgency. See Jason Lyall and Isaiah Wilson, III, "Rage Against the Machines: Explaining Outcomes in Counterinsurgency Wars," *International Organization*, Vol. 63, No. 1, Winter 2009.

[20] David E. Johnson, *Heavy Armor in the Future Security Environment*, Santa Monica, Calif.: RAND Corporation, OP-334-A, 2011b.

[21] Matthew Adam Kocher, Thomas B. Pepinsky, and Stathis N. Kalyvas, "Aerial Bombing and Counterinsurgency in the Vietnam War," *American Journal of Political Science*, Vol. 55, No. 2, April 2011; Monica Duffy Toft and Yuri M. Zhukov, "Denial and Punishment in the North Caucasus: Evaluating the Effectiveness of Coercive Counterinsurgency," *Journal of Peace Research*, Vol. 49, No. 6, 2012; Christopher Paul, Colin P.

Even if neutral observers might agree that highly discriminate targeting of irregular adversaries among civilian populations is extremely difficult, research suggests that local populations are unlikely to give outside actors such as the United States the benefit of the doubt when questions arise about their commitment to minimizing civilian deaths.[22]

In one sense, there is nothing unique to state-supported VNSAs about the challenges of discriminate targeting; irregular warfare almost inevitably generates high levels of deaths among noncombatants, at least when the insurgents are able to operate freely within the local population.[23] What is different is the level of capability that state support brings to irregular forces, with a concomitantly large need for actors like the United States to employ fires robustly.[24] In doing so, however, they run the risk of turning local opinion against them, thus strengthening the actors they sought to defeat. To the extent that hybrid actors mass their forces in an effort to seize and hold territory, they can be more easily targeted. But examples such as the Vietminh in the First Indochina War, the mujahideen in Afghanistan, and, more recently, Lebanese Hezbollah suggest that state-supported VNSAs can inflict heavy damage and sometimes even hold terrain while not presenting themselves as easy targets.

Clarke, and Beth Grill, *Victory Has a Thousand Fathers: Sources of Success in Counterinsurgency*, Santa Monica, Calif: RAND Corporation, MG-964-OSD, 2010; and Christopher Paul, Colin P. Clarke, Beth Grill, and Molly Dunigan, *Paths to Victory: Lessons from Modern Insurgencies*, Santa Monica, Calif.: RAND Corporation, RR-291/1-OSD, 2013.

[22] Jason Lyall, Graeme Blair, and Kosuke Imai, "Explaining Support for Combatants During Wartime: A Survey Experiment in Afghanistan," *American Political Science Review*, Vol. 107, No. 4, November 2013.

[23] Benjamin Valentino, Paul Huth and Dylan Balch-Lindsay, "'Draining the Sea': Mass Killing and Guerrilla Warfare," *International Organization*, Vol. 58, No. 2, Spring 2004.

[24] Johnson, 2010; Johnson; 2011; Bowers, 2012, p. 40.

Strategic-Level Challenges Posed by State Support to VNSAs

Various observers of military operations have suggested that the tactical- to operational-level challenges posed by hybrid opponents such as most state-supported VNSAs are difficult but manageable for highly competent militaries that prepare for both conventional and unconventional or irregular adversaries.[25] At the strategic level, the challenges posed by state-supported VNSAs are perhaps even more difficult to overcome.

Viability of Relying on Partners

The typically more-advanced capabilities of state-supported VNSAs can call into question the relevance of the OIR model, at least in the most challenging cases. Many VNSAs have been more than capable of defeating local actors, and some were capable of defeating major powers who intervened in their conflicts. As will be discussed in greater detail in Chapter 3, with the help of Communist China, the Vietminh were able to inflict repeated battlefield defeats on the French. Using wire-guided antitank missiles and Stinger antiaircraft missiles, the Afghan mujahideen outmatched the Kabul government and inflicted major losses on the Soviets. With Iranian support, Hezbollah is by far the most capable military actor in Lebanon. Similarly, as will be discussed in Chapter 6, the Iranian-backed Houthis are likely the strongest local actors in Yemen's civil war, despite Emirati and Saudi military support for Yemeni government forces. The fact that the French, Soviet, and Gulf Arab monarchies struggled against state-supported insurgents suggests that there may be future instances in which limited "by, with, and through" support on the model of OIR will be inadequate to prevent the defeat of U.S. allies or partners.

---

[25] Hoffman, 2009; Russell Glenn, *All Glory is Fleeting: Insights from the Second Lebanon War,* Santa Monica, Calif.: RAND Corporation, MG-708-1-JFCOM, 2012; Bowers, 2012.

Fighting for Time

If U.S. partners, even those backed by indirect forms of support such as the provision of materiel, intelligence, financial resources, and trainers and advisers, cannot achieve acceptable outcomes, the United States may find itself getting drawn into a more direct role in defending high-priority partners. In such cases, the United States may find it difficult to sustain its support for the time needed to bring the conflict to an acceptable end state.

Civil wars in general last a long time, approximately 15 years on average in the recent past.[26] Civil wars involving state support for the warring parties tend to last even longer than the average for all such wars.[27] The willingness of foreign states to deploy large numbers of forces in such wars, however, is much shorter—perhaps five to six years, on average.[28] There are only three cases—Vietnam, Afghanistan, and Iraq—in which the United States has deployed more than 25,000 troops (about one reinforced division) into an ongoing civil war. In each of these cases, the United States deployed forces on this scale for only six to eight years, much less than the 15-year average duration of civil wars. And even this six- to eight-year span may be overstating the United States' willingness to commit large numbers of forces. In Vietnam, for instance, there were only three years between when the United States started deploying forces in large numbers (1965) and the Tet Offensive (1968)—the point at which most observers believe the United States was committed to getting out of the war. Similarly, in Iraq, there were only three years between when the United States invaded (2003) and the

---

[26] James D. Fearon and David D. Laitin, "Ethnicity, Insurgency, and Civil War," *American Political Science Review*, Vol. 97, No. 1, 2003.

[27] On the duration of such wars, see, for instance, Aysegul Aydin and Patrick M. Regan, "Networks of Third-Party Interveners and Civil War Duration," *European Journal of International Relations*, Vol. 18, No. 3, 2011; Noel Anderson, "Competitive Intervention, Protracted Conflict, and the Global Prevalence of Civil War," *International Studies Quarterly*, Vol. 63, 2019; and Matthew Moore, "Selling to Both Sides: The Effects of Major Conventional Weapons Transfers on Civil War Severity and Duration," *International Interactions*, Vol. 38, No. 3, 2012.

[28] Stephen Watts, J. Michael Polich, and Derek Eaton, "Rapid Regeneration of Irregular Warfare Capacity," *Joint Force Quarterly*, No. 78, 3rd Quarter 2015.

introduction of the Surge, an effort to rapidly change the course of the war before domestic pressures to withdraw from Iraq became overwhelming.[29]

How can the United States (or other foreign supporters of embattled states) provide assistance for as long as it takes to bring a war to an acceptable conclusion while also trying to maintain domestic political support? In practice, the United States has typically used large numbers of forces to try to buy the local regime time in the early stages of an intervention before transitioning to a longer-term but much smaller residual force. This was the approach that the United States adopted in Afghanistan and Iraq, and it was the approach that the United States attempted to adopt in Vietnam through its policy of "Vietnamization" after Tet. Such an approach attempts to reconcile public sensitivity to casualties and other costs of seemingly intractable conflicts with the need to make a long-term commitment to fragile states.

State support for VNSAs complicates this approach. Because such militants are so much more lethal than typical VNSAs, they can potentially demand larger numbers of U.S. forces to counter and exact a much higher level of casualties on the United States. In prolonged conflicts without a clear path to victory, such costs can be extremely difficult for the United States to sustain politically.[30]

---

[29] Watts, Polich, and Eaton, 2015. State supporters of VNSAs may also have trouble sustaining their commitment over long periods of time, although the VNSAs themselves historically appear to have a greater willingness to fight for much longer durations. In the three cases in this report that involve external states supporting the counterinsurgents (government) in a war, the state supporters of the VNSAs all exhibited a willingness to provide support to the VNSAs for longer than the state supporters of the governments were willing to keep their troops deployed abroad.

[30] The United States has found it difficult to accept large numbers of casualties in cases where a clear path to victory is not evident to the American public. By reducing its footprint, it can potentially ease domestic pressures for withdrawal. On U.S. casualty-sensitivity, see Bruce W. Jentleson and Rebecca L. Britton, "Still Pretty Prudent: Post-Cold War American Public Opinion on the Use of Military Force," *Journal of Conflict Resolution*, Vol. 42, No. 4, August 1998; and Christopher Gelpi, Peter D. Feaver, and Jason Reifler. "Success Matters: Casualty Sensitivity and the War in Iraq," *International Security*, Vol. 30, No. 3, December 2005.

Sanctuary and Escalation

Numerous studies have highlighted the importance of sanctuary for insurgencies.[31] If a state is unwillingly hosting transnational VNSAs, those fighting the VNSAs can attempt to strengthen the capabilities of the host state if it is willing to take action against the VNSAs. If the sanctuary state is not willing to confront the VNSAs operating from its territory, then external actors such as the United States may attempt to coerce the sanctuary state into taking costly action that it otherwise would have avoided, or they might intervene directly to target the rebel sanctuaries. If the sanctuary state either has substantial military capabilities or is in alliance with states that do, however, then the options for eliminating sanctuaries decline dramatically. The Soviet Union, for instance, chose not to escalate its war in Afghanistan by seeking to eliminate mujahideen sanctuaries in Pakistan. As will be discussed in Chapter 4, the United States attempted to deny the Vietcong sanctuary and supplies from North Vietnam, but, fearing an escalation of the conflict into direct confrontation with China in particular, the United States limited the actions it was willing to take against Hanoi. Fears of escalation can also play out more subtly. It was highly unlikely, for instance, that any state would have directly militarily intervened in Ukraine to support the government against separatist forces in the Donbas region. But concerns over escalating tensions with Russia played a role in the United States' and other nations' reluctance to even provide lethal military aid.[32] Thus, state support to VNSAs can make it difficult to eliminate these militants' sanctuaries, making them much more difficult to degrade or defeat.

There are many historical examples of states either defeating state-supported VNSAs or at least fighting them to a draw. The governments of South Africa and Rhodesia, for instance, enjoyed considerable military success against a number of insurgencies in southern Africa in the 1970s and 1980s, despite these insurgents' support from the Soviets, Cubans, and

---

[31] Idean Salehyan, "Transnational Rebels: Neighboring States as Sanctuary for Rebel Groups," *World Politics*, Vol. 59, No. 2, January 2007; Jeffrey Record, "External Assistance: Enabler of Insurgent Success, *Parameters*, Autumn 2006; Ben Connable and Martin C. Libicki, *How Insurgencies End*, Santa Monica, Calif.: RAND Corporation, MG-965-MCIA, 2010.

[32] The Donbas War is examined in greater detail in Chapter 5.

others. Israel has succeeded in checking the damage that Hamas can inflict, despite Iranian support for the group. And the United States inflicted punishing losses on Iranian-backed militias in Iraq.[33] None of the challenges presented by state-supported VNSAs, then, is insuperable. As the cases in this report suggest, however, the challenges are daunting enough to demand the serious attention of U.S. defense planners—and potentially the commitment of resources to prepare the U.S. military specifically for these sorts of challenges.

Summary and Research Design

The literature review summarized in this chapter suggests that state support to VNSAs often greatly increases their military capabilities, and these increased capabilities, in turn, often cause these actors to adopt hybrid warfare practices when fighting highly capable militaries like that of the United States. With these two points as background, we draw on prior analyses to develop five propositions about the challenges that state-supported VNSAs may pose:

- State-supported VNSAs facing highly capable adversaries may undertake highly complex forms of combat operations by combining elements of conventional and irregular warfare, and these complexities may prove challenging for the leaders of the state militaries fighting them.
- The greater lethality of many state-supported VNSAs may introduce serious targeting and force protection dilemmas for the militaries fighting them. Specifically, this greater lethality may force them to reduce their own casualties through intensive use of standoff fires, even though doing so makes population-centric counterinsurgency extremely difficult. Alternatively, they may opt to accept greater

---

[33] David E. Johnson, Agnes Gereben Schaefer, Brenna Allen, Raphael S. Cohen, Gian Gentile, James Hoobler, Michael Schwille, Jerry M. Sollinger, and Sean M. Zeigler, *The U.S. Army and the Battle for Baghdad: Lessons Learned—And Still to Be Learned*, Santa Monica, Calif.: RAND Corporation, RR-3076-A, 2019.

casualties to conduct a population-centric campaign but thereby risk domestic political support for the war.

- Because of the greater lethality and other military capabilities often enjoyed by state-supported VNSAs, many government forces—sometimes even fairly capable ones—will be unable to stave off defeat without high levels of foreign support. For the most capable state-supported VNSAs, this fact will call into question the viability of the indirect or "by, with, and through" approaches on which the United States is currently depending to counter such threats.
- The greater lethality of many state-supported VNSAs may complicate U.S. efforts to sustain on-the-ground military support for an embattled partner government over long periods of time, even if the United States reduces its footprint to minimize its casualties.
- When VNSAs receive military support from an outside state with substantial capabilities, the threat of direct intervention by the outside power may greatly complicate U.S. efforts to eliminate sanctuary for the VNSAs or to escalate the conflict to a level that the VNSAs could not endure.

In the following four chapters, we examine four cases of conflict with state-supported VNSAs to determine whether the above propositions are borne out by the evidence in a wide range of cases. The four cases include the First Indochina War (in which France fought insurgents supported by Communist China), the Second Indochina War (in which South Vietnam and the United States fought a complex mix of insurgents and regular forces from North Vietnam), the Donbas War (in which the Ukrainian government fought surrogates armed and led by Russia), and the Houthi Rebellion (in which the Yemeni government, supported by a coalition led by Saudi Arabia, fought the Houthis).[34]

The purpose of this report is to better understand the military implications of such conflicts for the United States and, in particular, the U.S. Army.

---

[34] The latter two wars remain ongoing, so we cannot draw definitive conclusions about the outcomes of these wars. Our five propositions, however, focus on combat dynamics, not war outcomes. Sufficient evidence has accumulated over the course of several years for us to assess the combat dynamics in these ongoing conflicts.

The cases, therefore, were not chosen to be representative of the full range of state-supported VNSAs. Rather, the cases were selected to represent the sorts of VNSAs that might be most likely to pose military challenges to the U.S. Army (and, more broadly, all the U.S. military services). In social science terms, the cases were selected because they represented extreme values on the primary explanatory factor of interest—the state-provided military capabilities of the VNSAs (and, by extension, their ability to wage a highly challenging form of proxy warfare). While these cases are not representative of the full range of instances of state-supported VNSAs, they are likely reasonably representative of the sorts of cases in which a substantial number of U.S. ground forces might become involved. Using statistical analysis of historical conflicts, RAND researchers have found that the United States only engages in counterinsurgency on a large scale in the most challenging environments.[35] The United States has practiced large-scale counterinsurgency in the post–World War II era only in Vietnam, Afghanistan, and Iraq, all cases in which either state support of VNSAs or the collapse of the partner government (or both) made U.S. military operations particularly challenging.[36] While the United States has become involved in counterinsurgencies and proxy wars in less challenging circumstances, it has typically relied on Special Operations Forces, standoff airstrikes, intelligence and materiel support, or private military contractors—or some combination of these tools. Although these lesser contingencies may have important implications for U.S. foreign and security policy as a whole, they have less relevance for the conventional forces of the U.S. Army.

Despite not being representative of the full range of instances of proxy wars or the "average" case of state-supported VNSAs, these cases span multiple regions of the world, took place in the Cold War and post–Cold War eras, and include both ideological and what might be described as "ethnic" conflicts. Thus, while these cases represent particularly capable VNSAs, they occur in a broad range of contexts, suggesting that the conclusions we derive from our case studies may apply to other cases in which the U.S.

---

[35] Watts et al., 2017.

[36] Jennifer Kavanagh, Bryan Frederick, Matthew Povlock, Stacie L. Pettyjohn, Angela O'Mahony, Stephen Watts, Nathan Chandler, John Speed Meyers, and Eugeniu Han, *The Past, Present, and Future of U.S. Ground Interventions: Identifying Trends, Characteristics, and Signposts*, Santa Monica, Calif.: RAND Corporation, RR-1831-A, 2017.

Army might become involved on a large scale (though we cannot directly assess their generalizability without more research). Readers should bear in mind, however, that less-capable VNSAs are much more common, and the findings in this report may not be applicable to them.

These case studies of specific conflicts are based around three major questions:

- What capabilities did states provide to VNSAs that they otherwise would have been unlikely to acquire?
- What were the tactical- and operational-level military challenges that these state-supported VNSAs posed both to the local governments they fought and to any foreign forces engaged in intervention on behalf of the government?
- What were the strategic implications of state support for the course of the conflict? Did state support make VNSAs more militarily capable than the states that fought them (either the governments in the conflict-affected countries or foreign governments that intervened to support them)? Did these state-provided capabilities make it more difficult for external counterinsurgents to commit to long-term interventions? And did foreign support for VNSAs provide them sanctuary and/or limit options for escalation against them?

The ideal research design to analyze these questions would have involved assessing periods in each conflict before the VNSAs received state support and after, comparing the two periods to determine which additional military challenges were made possible by state support. In actual practice, such an analytic structure is challenging. In many cases there were no clear "before" and "after" periods; rather, state support varied throughout the conflict and, given its often-covert nature, is difficult to determine with precision. Moreover, because in many cases the VNSAs gained different military capabilities at different points in the conflict, the comparisons would have had to span multiple periods in each war. Such detailed comparisons were not feasible within the scope of this research. Instead, we sought wherever possible, through a combination of specific examples and expert judgments derived from secondary sources, to indicate the difference that state support made for the military capabilities of VNSAs and the tactical-, operational-, and strategic-level challenges that followed from those changes in capability.

CHAPTER 3

The First Indochina War: France and China in Vietnam

Introduction

In the aftermath of World War II, France became embroiled in fighting the Vietminh, an insurgency seeking to liberate Vietnam from French colonial control and establish a sovereign country. In fighting the Vietminh, France was faced with the dilemma of fighting both a popular insurgency based in the rugged jungles and a conventional force supported by a large industrial base. Vietminh guerillas occupied much of the countryside, causing a steady stream of casualties and forcing the French to disperse much of their military to defend logistical centers, lines of communication, and population centers. Even though the French controlled the great majority of the country's factories, Chinese training and military aid enabled the Vietminh to also field large, conventional formations that were often able to overmatch their French opponents on the field of battle. In the end, France's defeat was not inevitable; Paris still had command of substantial forces that it could have thrown in to counter the Vietnamese insurgency and its foreign-equipped conventional divisions. But France still had other interests in Europe and throughout its colonial empire that needed protecting and was unwilling to pay the very steep price that the Vietminh could impose with the help of their Chinese patrons.[1]

---

[1] Kevin Ruane, "Refusing to Pay the Price: British Foreign Policy and the Pursuit of Victory in Vietnam, 1952–1954," *English Historical Review,* Vol. 110, No. 435, February 1995, p. 77.

Although now many decades old, this case provides valuable insights into the questions posed at the end of the last chapter. First, it demonstrates the extent to which Chinese support to the Vietminh provided it with military capabilities vastly superior to what it otherwise would have had. Second, it illustrates the tactical- and operational-level military challenges that Chinese support to the Vietminh created for France and the difficulty France had in adapting to these challenges. Third, although we cannot know exactly how the war would have turned out in the absence of Chinese support, the case study helps to show how Chinese support greatly increased France's costs of continued fighting, ultimately leading to its withdrawal from the country.

Background

French Indochina (or, more formally, the Indochinese Union) was a colony of France from 1887 until its occupation by the Japanese in 1941. The Japanese eliminated many of the French institutions that had maintained social stability in the colony and brought about a terrible famine in northern and central Vietnam, leading to considerable popular discontent. To take advantage of these circumstances, Ho Chi Minh and the Vietnamese communists formed a broad, nationalist revolutionary military group called the Vietminh and began fighting the Japanese. Following Japan's surrender in 1945, both the French and the Vietminh rushed to seize control over the country. The French were able to establish control in the South, where a variety of secret societies and militias had provided alternative centers of power to the Vietminh and where the British facilitated the quick return of the French authorities. In the North, the nationalist Chinese turned control over to the Vietminh. As Ho scrambled to build his ragtag guerilla movement into a functioning state and military, French forces flowed into the region and began attacking the North. Paris was eager to regain its colonies to secure its great power status and believed that maintaining a foothold in Southeast

Asia would ensure it access to the natural resources of the region to rebuild its war-torn economy at home.[2]

Initially, the French had the upper hand. Their superior training and firepower, combined with the ineptitude of the Vietnamese in conventional operations, enabled them to rout the Vietminh forces and capture both their base areas and most of the cities of the North in their 1947 offensive.[3] By 1950, Ho was so dismayed at the performance of his own officers that he asked Beijing to send him Chinese officers to command Vietnamese regiments and battalions.[4] Despite these initial successes, the French soon stalled. With colonial revolts breaking out in Algeria and Madagascar, as well as the need to station troops in occupied Germany, Paris did not have enough men on the ground in Vietnam to capitalize on its early successes and either destroy Ho's military forces or to effectively control the population in the face of a determined and popular guerilla force.[5]

Not only were French forces stalling by the turn of the decade, but the Vietminh gained access to a critical new source of supplies. After defeating the nationalists in 1949, the Chinese Communist Party's (CCP's) central leadership began directing much greater support to the Vietminh. At the time, a triumphant Mao saw the Chinese revolution as just one part of a broader revolution against imperialism throughout Asia and believed that supporting revolutionaries abroad would make his new People's Republic of China both stronger and safer.[6] Mao also feared an imperialist invasion from the south and wanted a reliable revolutionary neighbor to help secure his southern flank.[7]

[2]   Mark Philip Bradley, *Vietnam at War*, New York: Oxford University Press, 2009, pp. 33–36, 38–39, 41–44.

[3]   Bradley, 2009, pp. 50–51.

[4]   Qiang Zhai, *China and the Vietnam Wars*, Chapel Hill, N.C.: University of North Carolina Press, 2000, p. 19.

[5]   Bradley, 2009, pp. 49–50; McCuen, 2008, p. 109.

[6]   Shen Zhihua and Xia Yafeng, "Leadership Transfer in the Asian Revolution: Mao Zedong and the Asian Cominform," *Cold War History*, Vol. 14, No. 2, 2014, pp. 212–213; Qiang, 2000, pp. 20–21.

[7]   Qiang, 2000, p. 20.

Chinese training and weapons enabled the Vietminh to field large, conventional formations of infantry, artillery, and antiaircraft guns. Vietminh insurgents throughout the country were still able to launch small-scale attacks to fix the French in place, while large, Chinese-trained conventional units overran all but the strongest French garrisons.[8] First to fall were the French fortresses along Route Coloniale 4, along the Sino-Vietnamese border.[9] Next came an unsuccessful attempt by the Vietminh to use their new conventional units to smash through French defenses around the Red River delta.[10] Mounting losses helped to sway the French public against the war, and by 1953, Paris was looking for a way to end the conflict.[11] In 1954, Vietminh divisions used imported trucks and cannons as well as domestic porters to smash the French garrison at Dien Bien Phu, paving the way for a French withdrawal following the 1954 Geneva peace conference.[12]

How State Support Enhanced the Capabilities of the Vietminh

Before 1949, Ho Chi Minh had already built a viable movement with capable leadership and broad public support that was able to produce and import basic infantry weaponry, though not in particularly massive quantities.[13] His armed forces, however, lacked the training or heavy weapons needed to engage in large-scale conventional operations, leading to many defeats at

[8]   Charles R. Shrader, *A War of Logistics: Parachutes and Porters in Indochina, 1945–1954*, Lexington, Ky.: University of Kentucky Press, 2015, p. 174.

[9]   Shrader, 2015, pp. 204–212.

[10]   Shrader, 2015, pp. 220–223.

[11]   James Cable, *The Geneva Conference of 1954 on Indochina*, New York: Springer, 1986, p. 15.

[12]   Ruane, 1995, pp. 84–86; Shrader, 2015, p. 343.

[13]   Joseph Jermiah Zasloff, *The Role of the Sanctuary in Insurgency: Communist China's Support to the Vietminh, 1946–1954*, Santa Monica, Calif.: RAND Corporation, RM-4618-PR, 1967, p. 73; Bradley, 2009, pp. 49–50.

the hands of the French.[14] Even before Mao Zedong's CCP and People's Liberation Army (PLA) won their own civil war in 1949, they began providing these services. While official contact between CCP central leadership and the Vietminh was spotty before the end of the Chinese civil war, Ho Chi Minh already had a long history of working with the CCP and had visited Mao in Yanan in 1938.[15] In 1946, Ho provided safe harbor within his territory for the CCP's Southern Guangdong People's Force, which was pushed out of southern China by Chinese nationalist forces. While sheltering in Vietnam, these units provided trainers for Vietnam's Advanced Infantry School and Cadre Training Center, as well as embedded trainers for units.[16]

Following the CCP's victory in the Chinese civil war, CCP leaders began to substantially increase China's aid to the Vietminh insurgency. PLA training helped turn the Vietminh armed forces from a ragtag collection of often incompetent small units into a professional, lethal fighting force. With PLA support, basic infantry training became much more common among the Vietminh forces.[17] In the early 1950s, most Vietnamese noncommissioned, regimental grade, and staff officers were trained in China, as were engineers, tankers, and other specialized troops, as many as 40,000 in all.[18] PLA officers, demolitionists, and gunners also went into Vietnam to provide training to specialists there.[19] In addition, the Vietnamese imported and translated large numbers of Chinese training manuals to train their forces at home.[20] When specialists were not available, Chinese trainers seem to have manned Vietnamese antiaircraft and artillery batteries themselves and perhaps even served as infantry, though it is difficult to determine how many Chinese advisers engaged in combat or what role they played.[21] At

---

[14] Bradley, 2009, pp. 48–49.

[15] Qiang, 2000, pp. 10–11.

[16] Qiang, 2000, p. 12.

[17] George Kilpatrick Tanham, *Communist Revolutionary Warfare: From the Vietminh to the Viet Cong*, Westport, Conn.: Praeger Security International, 2006, p. 31.

[18] Tanham, 2006. p. 33.

[19] Shen and Xia, 2014, p. 210.

[20] Shrader, 2015, p. 174.

[21] Shrader, 2015, pp. 174–176.

least 1,000 Chinese doctors served in Vietnam, making up for a critical shortfall in medical personnel in the Vietminh's ranks.[22]

After the decision to aid the Vietminh was made, the PLA began rapidly forming Vietnamese fighters into larger units. In 1950 alone, 2000 Vietnamese troops traveled to China where they were clothed, armed, trained, and formed into regiments before being sent back to Vietnam, a process that usually took about three months.[23] By the end of the war, the PLA had trained and equipped nine infantry divisions, one infantry regiment, two artillery regiments, and many local forces.[24] While the Vietminh deserve great credit for their guerilla campaign, the large conventional formations that defeated the French at Dien Bien Phu were to a great extent creations of the PLA.

Almost as important as Chinese training was the massive volume of supplies that Beijing provided the Vietminh. By 1952, the Chinese had supplied about 100,000 rifles, 5,200 machine guns, 650 heavy mortars, 170 recoilless rifles, more than 48 antiaircraft guns, and more than 66 artillery pieces.[25] These arms accounted for less than a quarter of Chinese aid, the majority of which consisted of petroleum products and ammunition. There is much disagreement over the exact weight of supplies provided at different phases of the war, but it seems that by 1954 China was providing around 1,500–4000 tons a month.[26] While China was far from the only source of weapons for the Vietminh, it was a key source of supplies without which the Vietminh may not have been able to force the French to capitulate.[27]

In addition to the essential training and equipment that the Chinese provided to their Vietminh allies, Mao Zedong's theories of people's war (which had recently been demonstrated successfully in the Chinese civil war) showed how a downtrodden and militarily inferior group of leftist revolu-

---

[22] Shrader, 2015, p. 176.

[23] Shrader, 2015, pp. 174–175.

[24] Shen and Xia, 2014, p. 210.

[25] Shrader, 2015, p. 168.

[26] Zasloff, 1967, p. v. Note that the French colonial government at the time provided significantly higher figures.

[27] Zasloff, 1967, p. v; Bradley, 2009, p. 66.

tionaries could defeat a much stronger foe. Strategically speaking, Vietnam broadly followed the recommendations of this theory by building secure base areas far from enemy forces; fighting the French to a stalemate in the countryside and destroying isolated outposts to secure control there; and finally launching a strategic, conventional counteroffensive.[28] The knowledge that these strategies had worked in China and the belief that they could work in Vietnam helped shore up Vietminh morale in the face of French military superiority.[29]

Military Challenges for France and Its Partners

Tactical Issues

Despite many tactical setbacks, Chinese training and materiel ultimately allowed the Vietnamese to defeat the French in large-scale, conventional battle. While Vietnamese strategists, soldiers, and porters all deserve credit for their victory at Dien Bien Phu, it is doubtful that they could have succeeded without Chinese artillery, antiaircraft guns, and munitions, much less Chinese training of regiments and divisions.[30] Though it took the Vietnamese regular forces some time to realize their potential, they were eventually able to build up a capacity to defeat their enemies in large combined-arms battles in the Vietnamese hinterlands.

Vietnam's first forays into large-scale conventional operations were admittedly disastrous. After the Vietminh's forces had successfully captured the French forts along the Chinese border, Vietnamese general Vo Nguyen Giap was eager to try his new divisions out against French forces guarding the Red River delta, one of the country's richest rice-growing regions.[31] In

---

[28] Bradley, 2009, pp. 35, 47–48. Note that there may have been some disagreement between the Vietnamese and the Chinese on the timing of these steps, and France's capitulation meant that the Vietnamese never had to actually recapture large cities like Hanoi. Nevertheless, the overall contour of the Vietminh campaign against the French was in many ways a classic Maoist revolution.

[29] Zasloff, 1967, p. 74.

[30] Shrader, 2015, pp. 165–166; Bradley, 2009, p. 66; Zasloff, 1967, p. v.

[31] Shrader, 2015, pp. 215–216.

these early battles, while the Vietnamese were often able to break through French lines, the French were able to maneuver sufficient force and firepower to meet and defeat them soon afterward.[32] Still, Vietnamese regular forces did prove sufficient to wipe out even very well-garrisoned and well-fortified outlying posts, forcing the French to cede key territory in the hinterlands.[33]

By 1954, the Vietminh had addressed many of the command staff and logistical problems that had hamstrung their 1951 conventional offensives.[34] Whereas in 1951 Giap had struggled to coordinate simultaneous operations around the Red River Delta, by 1954 he and his staff were able to coordinate large-scale offensives and guerilla action across Laos and Vietnam to occupy French forces and reduce the resources available to reinforce the French garrison at Dien Bien Phu.[35] While a lack of supplies stalled many of the advances in the Red River Delta campaign, by 1954 Giap had built a logistical planning staff and army of porters capable of supplying heavy artillery, heavy antiaircraft guns, and thousands of tons of ammunition (all of which came from Chinese factories), as well as supplies for tens of thousands of troops, to a remote mountain pass in the jungle.[36] Vietnamese engineers also managed to build and improve roads for hundreds of imported trucks to help in the logistical effort.[37] In the end, the Vietminh were able to field 24 105 mm howitzers, 15 75 mm guns, 30 37 mm antiaircraft cannons, and 100 smaller antiaircraft machine guns for the battle.[38] They managed to combine an insurgency's ability to move throughout the countryside over rough terrain with all the firepower of a conventional, industrialized war machine.

Chinese training in large-unit combat enabled the Vietnamese to field four divisions in and around the airfield and use their Chinese artillery and

[32] Shrader, 2015, p. 224.

[33] Shrader, 2015, pp. 209, 212–213.

[34] Shrader, 2015, p. 341.

[35] Shrader, 2015, pp. 307–308.

[36] Shrader, 2015, pp. 222, 349–350.

[37] Shrader, 2015, pp. 246–351.

[38] Shrader, 2015, p. 215.

antiaircraft guns (possibly manned by Chinese soldiers, given the dearth of Vietnamese soldiers capable of operating these complex weapons systems) to cut off the outpost from aerial resupply.[39] This force not only outnumbered the isolated French defenders but, with Chinese artillery in the hills around the outpost, it also managed to outgun them.[40] Although Dien Bien Phu was well prepared to fend off large infantry assaults, its vulnerability to artillery in the hills surrounding the base was recognized by outside observers. The French discounted the Vietminh's ability to field a large artillery force there, to their peril, and the garrison was crushed just as negotiations were beginning in Geneva to end the conflict.[41]

Operational Issues

Even without Chinese support, the Vietminh were able to build a highly capable and highly popular guerilla movement.[42] While most Chinese arms initially went to regular units, this freed up a much greater supply of arms for Vietminh guerilla forces, making them a more lethal force.[43] Not only were guerillas better armed, but Vietnamese regular troops could substantially augment them, holding French rear areas and lines of communication at risk. In 1954, Giap managed to infiltrate an entire division through French lines on the Red River Delta, endangering logistical bases and pinning French forces in place during the Dien Bien Phu campaign.[44]

Foreign support enabled the Vietminh to present the French (and later the Americans) with a dual dilemma. It made an already pervasive guerilla movement much more capable and deadly, providing it with massive supplies of fighters and weapons.[45] Both the French and the Americans recog-

---

[39] Shrader, 2015, pp. 321–322, 343, 176.

[40] Shrader, 2015, pp. 360–361.

[41] Shrader, 2015, p. 343.

[42] Zasloff, 1967, p. 73.

[43] Shrader, 2015, p. 180.

[44] Shrader, 2015, p. 311.

[45] Bradley, 2009, p. 147. While Vietnamese regulars never seemed to take as prominent a role in the guerilla struggle against the French as they did against the Americans after

nized that spreading out and occupying the countryside would be essential to prevent strangulation by guerilla forces and devoted considerable forces to those objectives.[46] At the same time, they could not ignore the large, capable conventional forces that foreign aid had enabled the Vietnamese Communists to amass. In the French case, even before Dien Bien Phu, Vietnamese conventional units with artillery support were able to destroy well-fortified positions garrisoned by thousands of soldiers.[47] Even large French forces were vulnerable if not massed in relatively close proximity to one another, and the French needed to concentrate their forces to launch attacks against Vietnamese conventional formations and their supply bases.

While Vietminh conventional forces were capable of inflicting much higher casualties on their French counterparts, like conventional forces everywhere, they were dependent on large supplies of materiel. Recognizing this, the French often tried to disrupt Vietnamese operations by capturing key supply depots or lines of communication. While these efforts caused hardship for the Vietnamese, they did not stop large-scale operations.[48] Likewise, French control over the most productive rice-growing regions

---

1968, the ability of the Vietminh to infiltrate an entire division of regular troops to aid local guerillas suggests that the existence of large regular units could substantially augment the capabilities and manpower of guerilla forces when deemed necessary. See Shrader, 2015, p. 311.

[46] Shrader, 2015, p. 190. Note that while some (most notably Harry G. Summers) have argued that the Vietcong guerilas in the South during the American war in Vietnam were more of a distraction than an enemy center of gravity which had to be destroyed, the political turmoil of the mid-1960s in South Vietnam suggests that if the insurgency had not been stemmed by an infusion of outside forces, it might have itself been sufficient to destroy the South Vietnamese government. Likewise for the French, while the guerilas were arguably not the true center of gravity of Vietminh forces, their effective raids on French roads and airfields deep within French fortified lines show that had the French not diverted some forces to defend their interior logistical bases and loyal populations, the Vietnamese could have quickly rendered the maintenance of a conventional force in the field all but impossible. See Harry G. Summers, *On Strategy*, New York: Presidio Press, 1995, p. 144; Bradley, 2009, pp. 97–98; and Shrader, 2015, p. 311.

[47] See, for example, the campaign to destroy the French fortresses along Route Coloniale 4 (Shrader, 2015, pp. 204–212).

[48] In Chapters 9 and 10, Shrader details several such operations, including Operation Lorraine and Operation Hirondelle.

of the country helped block the Vietminh's access to food and recruits.[49] Despite these efforts, the Vietnamese were still able to amass the supplies they needed to keep their conventional forces in the field.[50] While China was far from the only source of materiel for the Vietminh, it did provide a steady stream of weapons, ammunition, trucks, and petroleum products—supplies that require an industrial base and which would have been difficult for Giap's forces to gather through their insurgency networks. The Vietminh industrial base was in China and thus immune from French attack.

Not only did Vietminh insurgents draw French troops away from conventional battles, but they also hindered the movement of French forces around the country while facilitating the movement and concentration of Vietnamese units. The Vietnamese insurgency (often helped by detachments of regular soldiers) helped block roads throughout the country, significantly reducing the ability of the French to mass forces in response to Vietminh attacks.[51] In addition, guerilla control of the countryside enabled Giap to move large conventional units around the country undetected, enabling operational surprise.[52] Ultimately, the French proved unable to solve the dilemma of operating a dispersed counterinsurgency campaign at the same time as they tried to launch large, concentrated conventional attacks.[53]

Strategic Issues

Dien Bien Phu is famous for ending France's dominion in Indochina, but it should be remembered that, absent larger strategic factors, the battle itself may not have been decisive. The French still had thousands of troops in the country, and, just a few years earlier, they had proven their ability to defend

---

[49] Shrader, 2015, pp. 217–218.

[50] Note that the Vietminh did frequently run into supply problems, but these rarely halted operations. One exception was the conventional campaigns of 1951 around the Red River Delta, especially the Day River Campaign. See Shrader, 2015, pp. 220–223.

[51] Shrader, 2015, pp. 192–193, 288.

[52] Shrader, 2015, pp. 221–222.

[53] McCuen, 2008, p. 109.

the richest parts of Vietnam from Vietminh conventional attack.[54] Even so, war had become unpopular in France. Chinese intervention in 1950 promised to make the war longer and more costly, helping to turn the French populace against it, and by 1952, the French public and elites had begun clamoring for a negotiated end to the war, despite Paris's weak position in Indochina.[55] In 1953, Joseph Laniel was elected Prime Minister on a promise to bring the Indochinese war to a negotiated conclusion.[56] France's long slide into defeat at Dien Bien Phu spelled the end of its domination of Indochina not purely because it was a military disaster (though it was), but also because it came at a time when France was desperately trying to find a way to end the conflict and showed that the only way to prevent the Vietminh from dominating much of the country was substantial escalation, perhaps drawing in more countries and risking a wider war.[57]

Even without Chinese intervention on the side of the Vietnamese, it is possible that the war in Indochina could have devolved into a long contest of wills between Vietnamese insurgents and the French, and it is possible that the Vietnamese would have eventually prevailed. While the defense of Indochina was important to France and its western allies, it was generally not as important as the defense of Europe, and, by 1952, few were willing to divert significant forces away from Western Europe to defend French Vietnam.[58] Without foreign support, the Vietminh could possibly have continued to launch guerilla and terrorist attacks from their jungle bases to cause an endless drip of casualties to the French that would eventually have proven more than the French public was willing to support.[59] Still, if the Vietminh lacked Chinese-supported conventional forces, the French could have used a smaller force and spread it out to focus on counterinsurgency operations

---

[54] Shrader, 2015, pp. 223–226; Bradley, 2009, p. 60. Note that while Shrader and Bradley disagree on whether the 1951 offensive to capture the Red River Delta was a Chinese or Vietnamese idea, they agree that it was a disaster for the Vietnamese.

[55] Zasloff, 1967, p. VII; Ruane, 1995, p. 77.

[56] Cable, 1986, p. 15.

[57] Ruane, 1995, pp. 84–86.

[58] Ruane, 1995, p. 77.

[59] Shrader, 2015, p. 165.

and may have had time to build a viable, friendly state in Vietnam that could eventually take over the lion's share of the work. We cannot know for certain what costs the Vietminh could have imposed on the French without Chinese help or how long the French would have been willing to bear those costs. What we do know is that, with Chinese support, the Vietminh were able to defeat the French in conventional battles, forcing Paris and its allies to either substantially increase the number of their forces in Vietnam or to accept defeat. Given these options, France chose defeat.

Conclusion: The Strategic Cost of Operational and Tactical Losses

Although the Vietminh enjoyed deep support among parts of the population of Vietnam, Chinese support was necessary to make them the extremely effective fighting force they became. The Chinese wove disparate Vietnamese battalions into regiments and divisions and provided the training and weaponry that the Vietminh needed to field a conventional force. It may not be an exaggeration to say that the Vietnamese divisions that crushed the French at Dien Bien Phu were in many ways Chinese creations, albeit creations built of the excellent raw material provided by smaller Vietnamese units.

Chinese support created major military challenges at both the operational and strategic levels of war. Chinese arms aided Vietnamese insurgents in the countryside, where they pinned down French forces and enabled Giap to move his divisions freely. This gave the Vietnamese the ability to launch multidivisional, combined-arms attacks anywhere in the country and to consolidate their control outside of the narrow areas defended by the French. The French could perhaps have defeated this hybrid conventional and insurgent force if they had been willing to significantly increase the number of troops in the country to both drive the insurgents from the countryside and to fend off large-scale conventional attacks, but even that is far from certain. What is certain is that Ho Chi Minh's divisions defeated those of France on the field of battle, and Paris was unwilling to send more troops to continue to take the punishment he could inflict.

Ironically, Chinese help proved to be a two-edged sword. While Mao gave the Vietminh the tools they needed to defeat the French, he and the Soviets also deprived Ho of the ability to fully capitalize on his victory. By 1954, Beijing was exhausted by the Korean War, and Khrushchev had come to power in Moscow, promising to reduce tensions with the West.[60] Both capitals pressured the Vietnamese into accepting the division of their country, enabling forces allied to the West to remain in control of the South.[61] Although this arrangement angered many Vietnamese hardliners, others agreed that it was important not to press for immediate reunification of the entire country for fear of inciting American intervention. The Vietnamese leadership ultimately acquiesced to Chinese and Russian demands, accepting the partition of their country and setting the stage for the next war.[62]

---

[60] Shen and Xia, 2014, p. 212.

[61] Qiang, 2000, pp. 62–63.

[62] Bradley, 2009, pp. 67–68.

CHAPTER 4

The Second Indochina War: The United States in Vietnam

Introduction

Following the French withdrawal from Vietnam and the newly created country's bifurcation between North and South, South Vietnam was almost immediately beset by several antigovernment groups. While many of these were marginalized by government action, foreign organization, manpower, and materiel enabled the peasant-based, Communist National Liberation Front (NLF) to seriously threaten the Saigon regime.[1] In order to prevent South Vietnam from coming under Communist control, the United States dispatched combat troops to Vietnam in 1965. With the support of regular formations of the North Vietnamese Army (NVA) that had infiltrated the South, the NLF was able to inflict significant casualties on American and allied forces in South Vietnam, though it failed to ever decisively defeat them on the battlefield.[2] Even so, foreign sanctuary and support enabled

---

[1] Bradley, 2008, pp. 108–112, 126.

[2] In this chapter, the NLF is considered the proxy, fighting with the support of North Vietnam and other communist governments. Given the contested status of South Vietnam, however, clear divisions between state and nonstate actors and between interstate and intrastate conflict are hard to draw. As much as possible, we attempt to focus on the challenges posed by the NLF, while recognizing that direct participation of the NVA was one of the primary challenges to U.S. military operations and the key determinant of the final outcome of the war. For an analysis that emphasizes the centrality of the NVA, see Summers, 1982. (Even focusing solely on the NLF, this case differs somewhat from the others in this report in that the North Vietnamese intended to recapture and directly govern all of the South. In addition, the lack of ethnic differences between sup-

the insurgency to survive even devastating defeats at the hands of Washington and Saigon. Every time Hanoi's forces in the South were smashed, it was able to withdraw and rebuild them and then send them in for another attack. Eventually, the prospect of an interminable and bloody war proved unpalatable, even if it was bloodier for the Vietnamese than it was for the United States, and in 1973 all U.S. forces withdrew from the country. In 1975, Saigon fell, and the Vietnamese Communists realized their goal of reunification.

As with the prior case study, this analysis addresses three core issues. First, it documents the capabilities gained by the NLF through foreign support that it would not otherwise have had. Second, it reveals the tactical- and operational-level military challenges that foreign support posed to the United States. Finally, it shows how foreign support may have altered the course of the conflict by raising costs for the United States and limiting its escalation options.

Background

Despite their stunning victory at Dien Bien Phu, Ho Chi Minh's Vietminh were only able to gain formal control over the northern half of their country in the 1954 Geneva peace talks.[3] The southern half was ruled by the French-sponsored government, which fell under the control of Ngo Dinh Diem in 1955. The Geneva agreement called for elections in 1956 to form a unified Vietnamese government, but, fearing that he would lose a fair contest, Diem refused to hold any such national elections and instead began persecuting old Vietminh leaders who had remained in the South, along with any other political group which opposed him.[4] Diem's increasingly authoritarian government and mismanagement of the country made him extremely unpopular.[5]

---

porter and proxy facilitated close ties between actors, which helped to make the proxies a particularly effective force.)

[3] Bradley, 2008, pp. 67–68.

[4] Chen, 1995, p. 357.

[5] Bradley, 2008, pp. 97–98.

Throughout most of the late 1950s, North Vietnam remained hesitant to exploit Diem's unpopularity and foment revolution in the South. Hanoi was distracted with its own political and economic reforms at home, which caused significant social disruption, and its allies did not want to get dragged into another war in Indochina.[6] Even so, Diem's persecution of the Vietminh soon led to popular uprisings throughout the Mekong delta and other parts of the countryside, and Vietnamese Communists in the South clamored for the party in Hanoi to support and lead the insurrection.[7] While Hanoi was slow to provide its full backing to the movement, by 1959 it had started sending personnel to the South, mostly guerilla fighters from the South who had regrouped to the North as part of the Geneva ceasefire agreement. By 1962, the North Vietnamese Worker's Party infrastructure had penetrated even to the hamlet level in many places in South Vietnam.[8] Even with only minimal North Vietnamese support, the peasant movement was strong enough to force the South Vietnamese government out of much of the countryside.[9]

The incompetence and venality of Diem's government led to widespread peasant revolt in the countryside, and, by the mid-1960s, his actions had also alienated many in the cities. The Saigon government's oppression of the country's Buddhist majority generated intense resentment, leading to widespread urban protests in 1963.[10] By late 1963, both the South Vietnamese military and the United States had lost confidence in Diem, and disgruntled army officers killed him following a coup that November.[11] Instead of

---

[6] Bradley, 2009, p. 90.

[7] Bradley, 2009, pp. 90–91; See also David Hunt, *Vietnam's Southern Revolution: From Peasant Insurrection to Total War*, Amherst, Mass.: University of Massachusetts Press, 2008, p. 29. Note that while Hunt emphasizes that this was a popular uprising not directed from above and that North Vietnamese Worker Party officials were slow to take control over it, by 1962 it seems clear that the party and party members were leading the movement, even if they were not always perfectly loyal to directives from Hanoi. See Bradley, 2009, p. 43.

[8] Hunt, 2008, p. 43.

[9] Hunt, 2008, pp. 45–46.

[10] Bradley, 2009, pp. 101–102.

[11] Bradley, 2009, p. 104.

bringing stability and good government, the coup set off a series of military juntas and short-lived regimes that proved totally inadequate to stop the insurgency growing throughout the country.[12] The growing threat of the insurgency and the continuing collapse of the South Vietnamese government formed the backdrop of the U.S. decision to send combat troops to prop up the Saigon regime in 1965.[13]

Since 1959, Hanoi had steadily increased its level of support to the insurgency in the South, and that flow of men and materiel increased even more rapidly after the United States became involved.[14] This buildup culminated in the 1968 Tet Offensive, when the North Vietnamese military and its local insurgent proxies launched a massive assault on major cities and military bases across Vietnam.[15] Militarily, this campaign was a disaster. The Communists were unable to hold any of the positions they gained, and the casualties they incurred broke the back of the local insurgency.[16] Politically, however, images of dying Americans and knowledge that the Vietnamese Communists were able to launch an attack on this scale despite American efforts to subdue the insurgency helped turn American public opinion decidedly against the war.[17]

Following Tet, the United States began to withdraw its forces and to look for a face-saving way out of the war, while the North Vietnamese Army stepped up its infiltration into South Vietnam to compensate for the devastating casualties caused by the 1968 offensive.[18] In 1972, North Vietnam launched another major offensive against the Saigon government, this time consisting mostly of North Vietnamese regular infantry supported by tanks

---

[12] Bradley, 2009, pp. 104–105.

[13] William C. Gibbons, *The U.S. Government and the Vietnam War,* Princeton, N.J.: Princeton University Press, 1995, pp. 10–17.

[14] Qiang, 2000, p. 136; Michael Lee Lanning and Dan Cragg, *Inside the VC and the NVA,* New York: Fawcett Columbine, 1992, p. 111.

[15] Bradley, 2009, pp. 147–154.

[16] Bradley, 2009, p. 147.

[17] Summers, 1982, p. 134; Bradley, 2009, pp. 153–154.

[18] Bradley, 2009, pp. 147, 161–163.

and artillery.[19] This campaign was also a military disaster, inflicting massive casualties on the North Vietnamese, but Hanoi was able to make some territorial gains before signing a ceasefire agreement with the United States in 1973, resulting in the withdrawal of all American forces from Vietnam.[20] Soon thereafter, in 1975, North Vietnam launched a third major conventional offensive in South Vietnam, this time toppling the Saigon regime and paving the way for Vietnamese unification.[21]

How State Support Enhanced the Capabilities of the Vietcong

Foreign support for the Vietnamese Communist insurgency in South Vietnam was provided both by North Vietnam and by other Communist nations, mostly China and the Soviet Union. While the Chinese did make some attempts to establish more direct links with Indochinese insurgents outside North Vietnam's control, these were unsuccessful.[22] All foreign aid to the Communist insurgency ultimately went through Hanoi.

The aid provided by foreign countries to Hanoi for its struggle for reunification was substantial. With the exception of his sun helmet, almost every piece of equipment and weaponry used by a North Vietnamese regular infantryman was either produced outside of Vietnam or constructed using supplies from outside Vietnam.[23] China alone provided Vietnam with between 140,000 and 220,000 rifles, between 3,000 and 7,000 artillery pieces, and between 1,500 and 2,400 radios every year between 1965 and 1968.[24] After Brezhnev took over leadership of the Soviet Union, Moscow also began to provide large quantities of material aid, including advanced

---

[19] Stephen P. Randolph, *Powerful and Brutal Weapons: Nixon, Kissinger, and the Easter Offensive*, Cambridge, Mass.: Harvard University Press, 2007, p. 245.

[20] Bradley, 2009, p. 166; Qiang, 2000, pp. 204, 206.

[21] Bradley, 2009, pp. 170–174.

[22] Qiang, 2000, p. 175.

[23] Lanning and Cragg, 1992, pp. 103–104.

[24] Qiang, 2000, p. 136.

systems like anti-air missiles and tanks, which would become increasingly important as the North Vietnamese military became more mechanized and conventional.[25] While most of the weaponry provided was meant to equip light infantry formations and was not particularly dissimilar from arms that the insurgents could capture from South Vietnamese forces (with some exceptions, which are discussed in the tactics section below), the volume of weapons and ammunition imported from abroad enabled the insurgents and North Vietnamese Army (NVA) to field a much larger force in the South than would otherwise have been possible.[26] Ultimately, the Eastern Bloc acted as a practically unlimited arsenal, capable of supplying all of the needs of both the NVA and the South Vietnamese insurgency from factories that could not be touched by the American military.

The Chinese also provided hundreds of thousands of soldiers to build, maintain, and defend transportation routes into Vietnam. By 1969, more than 320,000 troops from the Chinese People's Liberation Army (PLA) had rotated into and out of Vietnam, freeing up thousands of Vietnamese troops for combat in the South and helping defend the country from American air attack.[27] The Chinese soldiers also helped to build roads, railroads, airbases, and fortifications to support Hanoi's war effort.[28] Although these troops were no doubt appreciated, their value in freeing up North Vietnamese manpower should not be exaggerated. Most Chinese troops were withdrawn in 1969 and 1970, and their absence did not prevent Vietnam from launching its massive 1972 Easter offensive.[29]

Perhaps the most important role of Chinese troops in North Vietnam was to signal to the United States that China would defend North Vietnam from invasion as it had defended North Korea. PLA troops in Vietnam made no attempt to hide their affiliation, possibly because their presence was meant to be seen by Washington.[30] Beijing repeatedly signaled to the

---

[25] Qiang, 2000, pp. 153, 178–179.

[26] Qiang, 2000, pp. 153, 178–179; Bradley, 2009, p. 108.

[27] Qiang, 2000, p. 135; Bradley, 2009, p. 112.

[28] Qiang, 2000, p. 135.

[29] Qiang, 2000, p. 137.

[30] Qiang, 2000, p. 138.

United States that, although it did not want another Korea-style conflict, it would send its armies to defend North Vietnam if America invaded.[31] For its part, Washington was also keen to avoid another direct conflict with Beijing. The fear of Chinse intervention limited the United States' willingness to bomb North Vietnam and ruled out any land invasion.[32] With Chinese protection, the NVA and its proxies would always have an inviolable sanctuary to which they could retreat and regroup and from which they could prosecute their war.

Initially, North Vietnam's contributions to the insurgency were relatively light, but they grew over time until the insurgency resembled a Northern invasion more than a Southern rebellion. The National Liberation Front (NLF) insurgency in South Vietnam in many ways began as a genuine popular uprising in the late 1950s. While the Vietnamese Worker's Party did begin infiltrating personnel into the South in 1959 to help organize and staff the insurgency, the majority of the revolutionaries were initially Southerners rebelling against the Diem government's abuses.[33] Even so, in the 1960s, the NLF increasingly came under Hanoi's control. Central party directives were not always implemented with perfect fidelity by cadres on the ground in the South, especially in the early years of the uprising.[34] However, the movement's leaders were party members, and while they were often granted great latitude in the execution of Hanoi's directives, they generally received their orders and policies from Hanoi.[35] Following the final triumph of the Communists in 1975, NLF leaders were sidelined by transplants from the North, and those who complained about their marginalization were jailed.

---

[31] Bradley, 2009, p. 111.

[32] Bradley, 2009, p. 111.

[33] Hunt, 2008, pp. 28–41.

[34] Hunt, 2008, p. 56.

[35] Hunt, 2008, pp. 39, 43. Note that while Hunt emphasizes the agency of peasants at the village and hamlet level and correctly notes that they often were much more aggressive than party authorities were comfortable with, most of the leaders of the movement that he mentions were party members. The sometimes failed to carry out directives from Hanoi, and peasants sometimes acted without their authorization, but Hanoi maintained control over the organizational structure of the NLF, and this control grew as the war dragged on, necessitating ever greater infusions of northern personnel.

Though it may be an oversimplification to call the NLF a mere tool of Hanoi, it did operate under the overall control of the North Vietnamese Worker's Party, and it was discarded when Hanoi no longer needed it.[36]

While the manpower for the 1968 Tet Offensive was provided mostly by revolutionaries from the South, the organization and coordination needed to orchestrate the nationwide attack came from Hanoi.[37] By 1967, most insurgents in the South were already armed with modern weapons provided by Communist nations via North Vietnam.[38] The NVA also provided formations of veteran, conventional troops for key battles, such as the attack on Hue.[39] Hanoi's leadership and organization combined with Eastern Bloc weaponry to enable the insurgents to launch large-scale attacks involving artillery and thousands of infantry on cities throughout the South.

The Tet Offensive was a watershed moment for all parties in the conflict. Its political consequences were largely responsible for a shift in American public opinion that ultimately knocked the United States out of the war.[40] Morale in the American military began to decline precipitously as well, resulting in widespread strife, insubordination, and drug use among the troops.[41] Tet's military consequences had also broken the back of the NLF. Guerilla units were decimated by American firepower as they launched open attacks on South Vietnam's cities, and the movement's underground organization revealed itself to lead an urban uprising that never materialized.[42] North Vietnam, on the other hand, had committed only limited personnel directly to the offensive, and emerged from Tet ready to continue the war.

After the Tet offensive, not only the weapons being used against American and allied forces but even the people using them were largely infiltrated from the North. When American firepower and a lack of public support

---

[36] Lanning and Cragg, 1992, pp. 241–243.

[37] Hunt, 2008, p. 215.

[38] Lanning and Cragg, 1992, p. 111.

[39] Eric Hammel, *Fire in the Streets: The Battle for Hue—Tet, 1968*, Pacifica, Calif.: Pacifica Press, 1991, pp. 29–31.

[40] Summers, 1982, p. 134; Bradley, 2009, pp. 153–154.

[41] Bradley, 2009, pp. 155–156.

[42] Bradley, 2009, p. 152; Hunt, 2008, p. 215.

gutted the NLF, the insurgency was able to continue because Hanoi injected an increasing number of its own troops into the fight, both as replacements to fill out the ranks of the NLF's guerilla formations and as conventional large-scale units.[43] Just four years after the Tet debacle, as the United States was desperately looking for a face-saving way out of Vietnam, the NVA was able to launch another massive campaign across the country in 1972, this time mostly with North Vietnamese conventional units, including tanks and artillery.[44] While some guerilla operatives continued to hold on in the countryside and proved effective at tying down some South Vietnamese units, the bulk of the fighting was done by the NVA.[45]

Finally, in considering the significance of aid given to the insurgents from Hanoi, it is useful to consider the fate of other groups that opposed Diem's government. Soon after Diem came to power, he was opposed by the Cao Dai and Hao Hoa religious sects (which had their own armies and controlled significant territory in the countryside), as well as the Binh Xuyen criminal organization.[46] During the first Indochina war, these groups benefited from the general chaos, as well as military aid and funding from the French, and were able to set up semi-independent "kingdoms" throughout South Vietnam.[47] After gaining control over the government, Diem cut off the flow of funds and military supplies that these groups were used to receiving. In 1955, he crushed and conquered the territory of all three groups, a task made easier by the fact that their own military forces were severely reduced by the lack of supplies.[48] In the mid-1960s, as the NLF was taking over much of the countryside, the country's Buddhists also launched

---

[43] Lanning and Cragg, 1992, p. 46.

[44] Randolph, 2007, p. 245.

[45] Ronald H. Spector, *After Tet*, New York: The Free Press, 1993, pp. 290–294; Randolph, 2007, p. 39.

[46] Bradley, 2009, pp. 81–82.

[47] Bernard B. Fall, "The Political-Religious Sects of Vietnam," *Pacific Affairs*, Vol. 28, No. 3, September 1955.

[48] Fall, 1955, pp. 251, 253; Bradley, 2009, pp. 82–83. Note that remnants of the sects remained, but their military and political power was broken.

a largely urban resistance campaign.[49] Though the Buddhist crisis contributed to Diem's fall, subsequent South Vietnamese governments were able to effectively suppress them, and the Buddhist movement ceased to present a political challenge to the regime after 1966.[50] In the end, only the NLF, with its access to nearly infinite weapons, ample manpower, national coordination, and sacrosanct sanctuary from Hanoi, was able to defeat the United States and its allies.

Military Challenges to U.S. and Allied Forces

Tactical Challenges

Support from North Vietnam to the insurgents and the deployment of regular forces in the South made the United States' adversaries much more lethal. Between 1965 and 1968, Communist forces in the South were increasingly armed with the most modern weapons the Eastern Bloc could provide, including the infamous AK-47 assault rifle and RPD light machine guns, all of which used the same ammunition to make logistics easier.[51] Hanoi also provided Soviet and Chinese 82mm mortars and rocket-propelled grenade launchers.[52] These weapons were usually provided first to more conventional, full-time units and then to local guerillas, but by 1967 all Vietcong (Vietnamese Communist) units were armed with modern infantry weapons.[53] This represented a substantial improvement over 1959, when many insurgent militants were armed only with fake rifles or noisemakers.[54] Perhaps most importantly, the majority of the ammunition used by Vietcong and NVA units in the South was imported, though some was produced in

---

[49] Bradley, 2009, pp. 101–102.

[50] Bradley, 2009, p. 126.

[51] Lanning and Cragg, 1992, pp. 105–106.

[52] Lanning and Cragg, 1992, pp. 107–108.

[53] Lanning and Cragg, 1992, p. 111.

[54] Hunt, 2008, p. 46. Note that despite their lack of military equipment, Hunt found that large peasant rebel groups were still quite effective at chasing government officials out of their villages.

jungle workshops.[55] While NLF and NVA fighters generally were very disciplined in conserving ammunition, even they consumed vast quantities of munitions in their large 1968, 1972, and 1975 offensives, and these campaigns would be impossible without substantial quantities of ammunition provided from abroad.[56]

Imported heavy weapons also helped the insurgents create tactical dilemmas for American and allied soldiers. Mortars, recoilless rifles, and later Soviet artillery rockets enabled Vietcong and NVA infiltrators to launch low-risk standoff attacks on American airfields and other bases, which were the most common type of attack on airfields.[57] Soviet and Chinese artillery rockets, which became available in 1966, were especially useful for these attacks because of their portability and long range.[58] These rockets were also often used as terror weapons to bombard civilian populations from kilometers away.[59] Imported indirect-fire weapons were usually used for fire support during infantry attacks or sapper raids.[60]

Eastern Bloc and Chinese weapons also held American and allied helicopters and planes at risk. Imported AK-47 assault rifles, machine guns, and antiaircraft guns proved deadly against aircraft, especially slow-moving helicopters.[61] Even more deadly were the combined Soviet surface-air missiles and foreign-made antiaircraft artillery that defended the Ho Chi Minh trail toward the end of America's involvement in the war.[62] By the end of the war, the United States had lost more than 5,000 helicopters and fixed-wing aircraft.[63]

---

[55] Lanning and Cragg, 1992, pp. 131–132.

[56] Lanning and Cragg, 1992, p. 132.

[57] Roger P. Fox, *Air Base Defense in the Republic of Vietnam, 1961–1973*, Washington, D.C.: Office of Air Force History, 1979, pp. 41–42.

[58] Fox, 1979, p. 42.

[59] Lanning and Cragg, 1992, p. 108.

[60] Fox, 1979, pp. 41–42.

[61] Carlo Kopp, "Are Helicopters Vulnerable?" *Australian Aviation*, March 2005, p. 61.

[62] Randolph, 2007, pp. 42–43.

[63] Les Throndson, "Combat Survivability with Advanced Aircraft Propulsion Development," *Journal of Aircraft*, Vol. 19, No. 11, November 1982, p. 915.

Foreign support for the insurgents was especially apparent during the major Communist campaigns of 1968 and 1972. In both of these offensives, the massive quantities of weapons and ammunition used by the Vietcong and NVA were provided from abroad, and they enabled the Communists to launch simultaneous conventional assaults throughout the country involving thousands of soldiers.[64] After the 1968 Tet offensive (which was launched mostly with Southern troops armed with foreign weapons) gutted the Communist-led NLF in the South, the North Vietnamese army began to take on a much greater role. An increasing percentage of the fighters in the South came from the NVA.[65] By the time of the 1972 offensive, the NVA were fielding more-advanced weapons systems, including tanks and heavy artillery, and were able to launch combined arms offensives on allied forces throughout the South. In the attack on An Loc, they fired more than 8,300 rounds of artillery into the city before launching a combined tank and infantry assault.[66]

Despite all this technology and heavy weaponry, the Vietnamese Communists never achieved more than limited tactical success in conventional battles against the Americans. They were never able to bring overwhelming conventional superiority to bear on the scale they did against the French at Dien Bien Phu and along Route Coloniale 4.[67] Soviet-provided tanks and shoulder-launched anti-air missiles gave the NVA an impressive array of conventional capabilities on paper, but, in 1972, North Vietnamese soldiers were still unused to these new weapons, and their lack of relevant experience, training, and tactics hampered their effectiveness.[68] The rifles, rockets, artillery, tanks, and bullets they received from the Eastern Bloc helped the Vietnamese Communists inflict significantly greater casualties on the Americans than would otherwise have been the case, and the troops they brought in allowed Hanoi to keep the insurgency alive after most of its base

---

[64] Lanning and Cragg, 1992, p. 132.

[65] Bradley, 2009, p. 147.

[66] Randolph, 2007, p. 245

[67] Hunt, 2008, p. 215; Randolph, 2007, p. 339.

[68] Randolph, 2007, pp. 38, 245.

in South Vietnam was destroyed. None of these advantages, however, gave them tactical dominance over allied forces until after the Americans left.

Operational Challenges

As with the French, foreign support for the Communist insurgency in the South presented the United States with a dilemma. Especially in the mid-1960s, the NLF insurgency posed a threat to the Saigon regime that could not be ignored.[69] In order to protect the South Vietnamese government from rebel attacks, help it regain control over its territory, and protect its own facilities from guerilla attack, the United States was forced to disperse forces throughout the country to secure population centers and find and destroy rebel groups. This dispersal siphoned troops away from more conventional large-scale operations and often held them in place. On the other hand, the need to concentrate troops to find and destroy larger units in turn reduced the number of soldiers available for counterinsurgency.[70]

As in the French war, insurgent control over large swaths of the South Vietnamese, Laotian, and Cambodian countryside also enabled the North Vietnamese and NLF to move and mass large conventional units anywhere in the country. This was never more apparent than during the Tet Offensive, when Communist forces were able to launch large-scale attacks with guerilla and regular infantry units against most major cities and military installations across the South.[71] To be fair, much of this capability was a result of North Vietnamese enclaves in Laos and Cambodia. Even after the South Vietnamese NLF was decimated in the 1968 Tet offensive, the North Vietnamese were still able to launch simultaneous large-scale conventional attacks on the north, middle, and south of South Vietnam, though they were unable to infiltrate as many troops into major Vietnamese cities as they had during Tet.[72] Even so, the guerilla movement was never completely

---

[69] Bradley, 2009, pp. 108–112.

[70] Keith F. Kopets, "The Combined Action Program: Vietnam," *Military Review*, July–August 2002, pp. 79–80.

[71] Bradley, 2009, p. 147.

[72] Bradley, 2009, p. 166; W. R. Baker, "The Easter Offensive of 1972: A Failure to Use Intelligence," originally in *Military Intelligence Professional Bulletin*, 1998, reprinted in

destroyed in the South Vietnamese countryside, where it continued to tie down allied forces and cause a steady drip of casualties.[73]

The insurgency also helped supply Communist conventional forces in South Vietnam. While the majority of the ammunition that they used was provided by foreign sponsors, some was manufactured in jungle workshops either in or near South Vietnam, as were many of the grenades, mines, and other explosives used by the Communists.[74] Perhaps even more importantly, the majority of the food consumed by both guerilla and conventional troops came from the South. Much of this was rice and other crops collected or purchased by local guerilla units.[75] Most of the other miscellaneous items used by the NLF and NVA in the South, including kerosene, flashlights, batteries, and typewriters, were also usually procured in the South, though NVA troops infiltrating from the North would carry some of these items with them.[76] Even with these efforts, the North Vietnamese had to bear the enormous burden of fielding and supplying hundreds of thousands of troops using austere logistical routes, but the task was made at least somewhat easier by their southern proxies.

While the North Vietnamese were able to use their guerilla proxies to tie down enemy forces and to concentrate their own forces for decisive battles, they were unable to impair the ability of the Americans to mass their own forces for specific operations. With its large fleet of fixed-wing and rotary aircraft, the United States proved able to concentrate large forces and launch conventional operations anywhere in the country.[77] Even though the United States was able to bring to bear much greater military resources than the French, the same dilemma of mass versus dispersion challenged the United States. In many cases, the United States substituted what is often called the "lavish" use of firepower for manpower that was never sufficient. This heavy

---

Small Wars Journal.

[73] Summers, 1993, pp. 290–294.

[74] Lee and Cragg, 1992, pp. 110–111, 131–132; Bradley, 2009, p. 49.

[75] Lee and Cragg, 1992, pp. 112–113.

[76] Lee and Cragg, 1992, pp. 131–132.

[77] Andrew Wiest and Chris McNab, *The Vietnam War*, New York: Cavendish Square Publishing, 2016, pp. 59–66; Summers, 1993, p. 133.

reliance on firepower, in turn, helped turn local opinion against the United States and the Saigon regime.[78]

Every time the NLF or NVA massed conventional units for a large-scale operation, and even when they launched these operations across the entire country, they were never able to mass greater combat power than the Americans and their allies could mass in response.[79] For all of the advantages that having a proxy insurgency provided conventional forces, and for all of the added punch and protection that conventional forces provided the insurgents, the Vietnamese Communists were never able to mass enough combat power to deliver crushing operational or tactical blows as they had in the war against the French. In the end, there was no American Dien Bien Phu. On the other hand, such a decisive military victory proved to be unnecessary.

Strategic Challenges

While the large-scale conventional campaigns that foreign support made possible for the South Vietnamese insurgency were always militarily disastrous, they proved politically decisive. As noted above, although Tet was a failure on the streets of Saigon, it was successful in the halls of Washington, where it crushed Lyndon Johnson's hopes for reelection and helped shift the narrative from how to win the war to how to escape it.[80] While the tactical and operational advantages that the insurgents derived from foreign support were not enough to inflict decisive military defeats on the Americans, they were enough to make American victories much more costly.

Just as important as the insurgency's ability to make victory more costly for the United States was its ability to survive defeat. While the Tet Offensive was a major factor sapping America's will to fight, it also broke the back of the South Vietnamese NLF insurgency.[81] The NLF was so weakened that it is possible that without Hanoi's support, the Saigon regime could have defeated it after 1968 even without American intervention. Instead, the

---

[78] Kocher, Pepinsky, and Kalyvas, 2011.

[79] Hunt, 2009, p. 152; Randolph, 2007, p. 339.

[80] Bradley, 2009, pp. 153–154.

[81] Hunt, 2009, p. 215; Bradley, 2009, p. 147.

NVA made good the NLF's losses, and again threatened the Saigon government with ruin in 1972.[82] Foreign support was important not just because it made Tet possible. It was also important because it enabled the insurgency and its sponsors to launch two more major campaigns in 1972 and 1975 after suffering a crippling defeat. In short, the United States was not able to simultaneously commit enough forces to prevent the defeat of the Saigon regime and to maintain that commitment over long periods.

In a study of 30 insurgencies since 1978, RAND researchers found that in every instance in which counterinsurgency forces were successful, they managed to disrupt the insurgent's supply of personnel, materiel, financing, intelligence, or sanctuary. Counterinsurgency movements that failed to do so were unsuccessful, even if the insurgency lacked popular support.[83] In the Vietnam war, Soviet and Chinese aid provided Hanoi with a practically limitless supply of arms, and North Vietnam's own population provided a practically limitless supply of people for the insurgency in the South. Even after suffering 100,000 casualties among its own troops in the 1972 Easter offensive, Hanoi was still ready to launch another major campaign in 1975 to unify the country.[84] While these losses sometimes forced the Vietnamese to postpone plans for future operations, North Vietnamese formations were usually able to retreat to their sanctuaries in Laos, Cambodia, and North Vietnam to escape complete annihilation.[85] American attempts to isolate the Communist forces in the South by cutting supply lines through Laos and Cambodia inflicted significant casualties but never succeeded in cutting the insurgency off from these sources of refuge and supply.[86] Meanwhile, the United States remained unable to destroy the bulk of the North Vietnamese military or civilian infrastructure, because it was unwilling to risk war with China by invading North Vietnam.[87] The United States and

---

[82] Randolph, 2007, p. 339.

[83] Randolph, 2007, p. 339.

[84] Qiang, 2000, p. 204.

[85] Wiest and McNab, 2016, pp. 59–66, 148; Bradley, 2009, p. 166.

[86] Randolph, 2007, pp. 42–46.

[87] Summers, 1982, p. 129.

its allies could defeat every major offensive that Hanoi launched, but they could never prevent Hanoi from launching the next offensive.

Conclusion: Hanoi Was Willing to Lose for Longer Than the United States Was Willing to Win

Once again, state support for the insurgents was critical to making them a force capable of imposing high costs on the intervening U.S. forces. Chinese and especially Soviet factories provided the insurgents with many tools that they otherwise would not have possessed, and these capabilities enabled them to threaten aircraft, launch standoff attacks, and pose a much greater threat to American and allied soldiers. Perhaps even more importantly, the massive influx of infantry weapons enabled Hanoi to arm enough troops both in the Southern insurgency and in its own military to launch simultaneous, large-scale attacks across the south. Hanoi provided the leadership that enabled the insurgency to coordinate both guerilla and conventional operations to great effect, causing a steady stream of casualties and tying down American forces across South Vietnam. All these capabilities enabled the Vietnamese insurgents to inflict much greater casualties on the United States than would otherwise have been the case. Despite all these advantages, however, the United States and its allies remained superior on the conventional battlefield. While Hanoi's ability to maneuver and mass troops at will throughout South Vietnam could lead to temporary victories, the insurgents and their sponsors could never overcome the United States' ability to use its mechanized military and air force to bring overwhelming combat power to bear in response to Vietnamese threats anywhere in the country.

As suggested in Chapter 2, the relatively high levels of military capabilities possessed by the Vietcong (and the NVA forces supporting them) posed numerous dilemmas for the United States. The United States found it extremely difficult to simultaneously prosecute the conventional and irregular components of the Vietnam War.[88] In using "lavish" firepower to com-

---

[88] Krepinevich, 1986.

pensate for manpower shortages, the United States alienated much of the local population.

While the tactical and operational advantages the South Vietnamese insurgency derived from its foreign patrons were not decisive on the battle-field, they caused enough casualties to undermine U.S. domestic support for the war. Equally important was the fact that the factories of China and the Soviet Union and the population of North Vietnam ensured that Hanoi was always able to replace its losses even after devastating defeats. Chinese promises of protection put the North Vietnamese centers of gravity—their military, their economy, and their government—largely beyond the reach of the U.S. military unless it was willing to accept the risk of escalation to direct conflict with the Soviets and Chinese. The United States never lost the ability to mass unparalleled firepower and manpower anywhere in Viet-nam. The problem was that it had no way to mass its forces against Hanoi's war-making potential. All it could do was mass and defeat any offensive that Hanoi launched and hope that the insurgents would tire of being defeated before America grew tired of bearing the cost of defeating them—a hope that, of course, proved ill founded. The combination of the high costs posed by militarily capable Vietcong and NVA forces operating in South Vietnam and the limitations imposed by the U.S. fear of escalation to broader inter-state war left the United States in a strategically untenable position. Even if the government of South Vietnam could ultimately have taken over the counterinsurgency effort without large levels of U.S. support, the United States was unable to sustain the level of support necessary to protect it from direct assault by NVA forces, and reunification of the country was impor-tant enough to Hanoi that North Vietnam was willing to sustain losses and continue the fight indefinitely.

It is possible that even in the absence of support from Hanoi, the insur-gents could have proven resilient enough and eventually caused enough casualties to make the Americans leave, but this is far from certain. As noted above, the Saigon regime proved quite adept at crushing armed insur-gences that did not have foreign support in the 1950s.[89] In the 1960s, the Saigon government's corruption continued to alienate many, but even large

---

[89] Fall, 1955, pp. 251, 253; Bradley, 2009, pp. 82–83.

protest movements with support from many social strata (but without much help from Hanoi) were brutally crushed by the South Vietnamese military.[90] While the Saigon government certainly had its struggles, it may have been able to defeat or at least contain at relatively low levels of violence a purely domestic insurgency with some support from Washington. Under such conditions, U.S. support might have proven cheap enough for the United States to maintain for as long as necessary.

American reluctance to bear the costs of continuing to win in Vietnam is understandable. While Hanoi could afford to focus all of its efforts on reunification, Washington had to husband its strength to protect a variety of interests around the globe. The fact that the United States did not have any vital interest in the country is evidenced by the fact that after Saigon fell, the United States' global position was not seriously compromised. While the loss was embarrassing and led quickly to all of Indochina coming under Hanoi's control, other countries in the region (including North Vietnam's one-time ally China) quickly moved to contain Hanoi.[91] Once the North Vietnamese Communists gained control over all of Vietnam, they became embroiled in their own quagmire after invading neighboring Cambodia and trying to prop up a friendly government there as China and other powers supported an insurgency. There is a certain irony that while Hanoi was able to strategically outmaneuver the tactically superior Americans, it quickly became the victim of tactically inferior forces in Cambodia who were able to marginalize it strategically.

---

[90] Bradley, 2009, pp. 116–118, 125.

[91] Qiang, 2000, pp. 208–215.

CHAPTER 5

The Donbas War: Russia in Ukraine (2014–2020)

Introduction

This case study in the military implications of modern, high-end proxy warfare examines three questions. First, in what ways and to what degrees did Russian support to proxy agents in Eastern Ukraine before Russia's large-scale, overt invasion in 2022 provide VNSAs there with capabilities that they otherwise would not have had? Second, what tactical- and operational-level military challenges did Russian support to proxies in Donbas create for the Ukrainian government forces they fought, and how difficult was it for the Armed Forces of Ukraine (AFU) to adapt to these battlefield challenges? Third, what were the strategic-level effects of Russian support to VNSAs in Eastern Ukraine between 2014 and its large-scale invasion in 2022, and how might these strategic outcomes have differed in the absence of assistance from Moscow?

Background

The proxy war initiated in Donbas after Ukraine's 2013–2014 Maidan Revolution was, at its core, a manifestation of a divide, both domestic and international, over the country's geostrategic orientation and post–Cold War drift toward deeper integration into Western economic, political, and security institutions. Catalyzing the crisis, on November 21, 2013, pro-Russian Ukrainian president Viktor Yanukovych abruptly abandoned historic talks on an economic trade pact and political association agreement, which would have codified greater Ukrainian integration with the European Union (EU) under its Eastern Partnership Program.[1] Organically, peaceful pro-Western protests immediately materialized in areas of central Kyiv surrounding Maidan ("Independence") Square. Over the next three months, the popular movement escalated into episodic violence and riots, as dozens were killed and thousands injured in confrontations with state security forces. Finally, after a major spasm of violence in the capital on February 22, 2014, Yanukovych fled to exile in Russia, and a pro-Western interim government was formed in Kyiv. The next day, the Ukrainian Parliament (Rada) voted to cease recognition of Russian as the dual national language of the country, a significant political act that the Kremlin seized upon to propagate the narrative that the "rights and lives" of the majority ethnic-Russian population in Eastern Ukraine were in imminent danger.[2] Realizing an opportunity to redirect Ukraine's Westward trajectory toward Russia's geostrategic orbit, in late February–early March 2014, Russian special forces, naval infantry, and elite airborne troops covertly seized control of and quickly annexed the Crimean Peninsula, precipitating a second crisis beyond the capital and arousing serious security concerns within the Transatlantic Alliance.[3]

Backgrounded against these unfolding events in Kyiv and Crimea, in February 2014, Moscow initiated an overlapping, albeit distinct, covert political warfare program targeting the majority pro-Russian regions of Donetsk and Luhansk in Eastern Ukraine. Here, the Kremlin sought to destabilize the security and political situation to coerce the pro-Western interim government in Kyiv to devolve central power and accept a federalist system in which the pro-Russian eastern regions enjoyed greater autono-

---

[1] Wojciech Kononczuk, "Ukraine Withdraws from Signing the Association Agreement in Vilnius: The Motives and Implications," Warsaw, Poland: Centre for Eastern Studies, November 27, 2013.

[2] Bridget Kendall, "Crimea Crisis: Russian President Putin's Speech Annotated," BBC News, March 19, 2014.

[3] For a detailed treatment of Russian operations in Crimea in early 2014, see Michael Kofman, Katya Migacheva, Brian Nichiporuk, Andrew Radin, Olesya Tkacheva, and Jenny Oberholtzer, *Lessons from Russia's Operations in Crimea and Eastern Ukraine*, Santa Monica, Calif.: RAND Corporation, RR-1498-A, 2017, pp. 5–32.

my.[4] Paralleling the original goals of these protestors in Donbas, Moscow's "active measures" did not initially aim at secession and annexation. That is, while Moscow did "inspire, fuel, and perpetuate" the grassroots movement, it did not initially orchestrate it, nor immediately "give the green light" to rise up violently.[5]

Mimicking the Maidan protestors' playbook, in early March 2014, this first generation of VNSA leaders in Donbas seized government buildings throughout the region before soon being arrested and replaced by a second generation with closer existing networks and linkages to the Kremlin and Russian security services.[6] The primary benefactors of Russian patronage thus became a diverse cast of powerful oligarchs and shady businessmen, "fringe" politicians and political organizations, and local "criminal elements" and nonstate paramilitary groups, all with divergent sets of self-interests and agendas.[7] As one RAND report explained, this critical juncture marked "the true beginning of the separatist movement and the transition from political warfare to insurgency . . . [after which] the conflict quickly escalated, arguably beyond Moscow's ability to control events."[8] Within the Kremlin, a schism reportedly formed "between 'doves' who doubted that the Crimea scenario would work in Donbas and 'hawks' who believed that Russia could count on local mobilisation to help oust Ukrainian forces and then annex as many as six eastern Ukrainian regions."[9] On April 7, the Donetsk People's Republic (DNR) announced its independence, followed a few weeks later by a similar declaration by the Luhansk People's Republic (LNR), officially marking a shift from the initial goal of federalization and greater political autonomy to outright secession and annexation by Russia.

---

[4] Keith B. Payne and John S. Foster, "Russian Strategy: Expansion, Crisis, and Conflict," *Comparative Strategy*, Vol. 36, No. 1, 2017.

[5] International Crisis Group, "Rebels Without a Cause: Russia's Proxies in Eastern Ukraine," Report No. 254, July 16, 2019, p. 3.

[6] Tom Balmforth, "A Guide to the Separatists of Eastern Ukraine," Radio Free Europe/Radio Liberty, June 3, 2014; Kofman, et al., 2017, p. 57.

[7] Kofman et al., 2017, pp. xiii, 55–60.

[8] Kofman et al., 2017, pp. xiii, 38–39, 55–56.

[9] International Crisis Group, 2019, pp. 2–3.

In the opening weeks of outright proxy warfare, the AFU proved both unwilling and unable to employ force against their fellow countrymen in Donbas, as thousands of servicemembers and local police defected to the insurgency. However, as the pace and degree of Russian support escalated with the introduction of heavy and advanced conventional weaponry and special operators in the late spring and early summer of 2014, the Ukrainian government successfully adapted, mounting a more coherent resistance. Subsequently, these AFU offensives "escalated the conflict vertically for Russia," and, with their irregular proxy forces on the precipice of defeat, this resulted in the transition to conventional warfare as Russian forces invaded with several thousand regular ground troops in August 2014.[10] During the conflict's first six months, the Kremlin's proxy strategy thus "cycled through four different types of warfare: political, irregular, hybrid, and conventional."[11] While persistently denying its involvement as a combatant, beginning with the Battle of Ilovaisk, Moscow continued to launch a series of large-scale conventional combat operations against the AFU alongside its proxy forces in Donbas until February 2015.[12] As the Minsk peace agreements slowly proceeded beginning in September 2014, the proxy war in Eastern Ukraine essentially ground to a stalemate along a 500-kilometer military line of contact, though the conflict has been prone to cyclical offensives and bursts of greater intensity.[13] More recently, as discussed in detail below, Moscow has moderated its end goal of annexing Donbas, creating fractures both within VNSA leadership ranks and between the insurgents and their benefactors in Russia.[14]

---

[10] Kofman et al., 2017, pp. 40–44, 69.

[11] Kofman et al., 2017, p. 69.

[12] Oksana Grytsenko, "Thousands of Russian Soldiers Fought at Ilovaisk, Around a Hundred Were Killed," *Kyiv Post*, April 6, 2018; Holcomb, 2017, p. 8.

[13] As Lawrence Freedman writes, the human and economic costs during the first six months of high-intensity fighting "were sufficient to create a desire for a cease-fire, but not the conditions necessary for a long-term settlement that could satisfy the key players. Without a settlement, a cease-fire became hard to sustain, so it became preferable to live with the conflict than make irrevocable compromises" (Lawrence Freedman, "Ukraine and the Art of Exhaustion," *War on the Rocks*, August 11, 2015).

[14] International Crisis Group, 2019, pp. i–ii.

In summary, in initiating a proxy war in Donbas, the Kremlin's strategic objectives were at least sixfold. First, as noted above, Russia sought to drive a wedge between Ukraine and the West and to prevent or delay its deepening integration into EU and North Atlantic Treaty Organization (NATO) institutions; more broadly, the Kremlin sought to "break Western unity" within these structures.[15] Second, while weakening Western power in its near abroad, Moscow simultaneously aimed to increase its own political and economic influence in this orbit by forcing Kyiv to accept some degree of federalization and devolution of power in Eastern Ukraine.[16] Third, Moscow's international security concerns and geostrategic threat perceptions placed a primacy on "retaining [geographic] buffers between itself and NATO" and ensuring basing access for its Black Sea Fleet in Sevastopol.[17] Fourth, while some observers in the West have somewhat cynically dismissed Putin's self-professed humanitarian motives for intervention— namely, to protect the Russian population in Ukraine and to respect their rights to self-determination—these concerns may well have been at least as partial explanatory factors for Russian state behavior.[18] Fifth, ideologically, much scholarship has cast Putin's return to proxy warfare in Eastern Ukraine as driven by revisionist, irredentist imperialist goals, a "new grand strategy" aimed at restoring Russian prestige lost at the end of the Cold War by "gradually recaptur[ing] the former territories of the Soviet Union" and projecting "Russia as a mighty and feared force to be reckoned with on the international stage."[19] Finally, some evidence suggests that economic ends

---

[15] Daniel Treisman, "Why Putin Took Crimea: The Gambler in the Kremlin," *Foreign Affairs*, May–June 2016; Frederick Kagan, Nataliya Bugayova, and Jennifer Cafarella, "Confronting the Russian Challenge: A New Approach for the U.S.," Institute for the Study of War, June 2019, pp. 25–26.

[16] Payne and Foster, 2017; International Crisis Group, 2019, pp. 2–3; Kofman et al., 2017, p. ix.

[17] Dylan Lee Lehrke, Miko Vranic, and Reed Foster, "Cold War II? Understanding the Balance of Power and Proxy Wars Between NATO and Russia," *Jane's Intelligence Briefing*, August 8, 2019, p. 18.

[18] Kendall, 2014; International Crisis Group, 2019, p. 3; Treisman, 2016.

[19] Anton Barbashin and Hannah Thoburn, "Putin's Brain: Alexander Dugin and the Philosophy Behind Putin's Invasion of Crimea," *Foreign Affairs,* March 31, 2014;

undergirded the Kremlin's political warfare means; in essence, the Maidan Revolution "threatened Putin's long-held plans to dominate the states of the former Soviet Union via an economically viable and politically subordinate Eurasian Economic Union."[20]

How Russian Support Enhanced VNSA Capabilities

Given the covert nature of ongoing Russian support to Ukrainian rebels, assessing precise levels of aid is of course impossible, especially in the unclassified domain. What is clear in the public record is that "Russia's proxy forces could not continue to fight without the support of the Kremlin."[21] Indeed, from early 2014 up to the point of large-scale invasion in early 2022, Russia flexed its proxy warfare capabilities in Donbas across nearly the full spectrum of types of military, economic, and political aid available in Moscow's toolkit. In the subsections to follow, we review seven types of Russian support: manpower, lethal weaponry, nonlethal equipment and materiel, cyber warfare, information warfare, direct financial support, and diplomatic-political capital. Table 5.1 summarizes all seven types.

Nataliya Bugayova, "How We Got Here with Russia: The Kremlin's Worldview," Institute for the Study of War, March 2019, pp. 21–23; Kagan et al., 2019, pp. 26–30.

[20] Alya Shandra and Robert Seely, "The Surkov Leaks: The Inner Workings of Russia's Hybrid War in Ukraine," *RUSI Occasional Paper*, July 2019, pp. 31–32; Franklin Holcomb, "The Kremlin's Irregular Army: Ukrainian Separatist Order of Battle," *Institute for the Study of War, Russian and Ukraine Security Report No. 3*, September 2017, p. 7.

[21] Holcomb, 2017, pp. 9–11.

TABLE 5.1

Summary of Russian External Support to VNSAs in Eastern Ukraine Since 2014

Category	Subcategory	Summarized Levels of External Russian Support
Manpower	Russian special forces	Peak estimate: ~700–2,000 Spetnaz/GRU troops
	Russian regular forces	Peak estimate: ~3,600–9,000 regular troops (in Donbas)
	PMCs	Unknown number; peak Wagner PMC forces estimated at ~5,000
	Other foreign fighters	Unknown number of Russian mercenaries, including Cossack bands, Orthodox Christian radicals, Russian nationalists, communists
Lethal materiel	Main battle tanks (MBT)	T-64 MBT; T-90 MBT; T-72B3 MBT
	Infantry fighting vehicles	BTR-82A; BTR-82AM
	Mechanized artillery	BMD-1; BMD-2; BTR-60; BTR-70; BTR-80; MT-LB towed howitzers
	Short-range air defense weaponry	Pantsir S-1 ADS; 2B26 Grad MLRS; 57E6 missiles; 2S9 Nona self-propelled heavy mortars; 2S1 Gvozdika, 2S19 Msta-S self-propelled howitzers; Strela-10M short-range systems and antiaircraft cannons
	Light/portable arms and weaponry	Various types of small arms, landmines, heavy flamethrowers, man-portable air-defense systems, rocket launchers; ATGMs

Table 5.1—Continued

Category	Subcategory	Summarized Levels of External Russian Support
Nonlethal materiel	Unmanned aerial vehicles	Orlan-10-, Granat-4-, Zastava-, and Tachion-type unmanned aerial vehicles (UAVs)
	Armored personnel carriers	BMP-2 and BPM-97 armored personnel carriers
	Mobile radar, C2 systems	1L271 Aistonok system; Kamaz-43269 "Dozor" armored command and control (C2) vehicle
	Electronic warfare (EW) systems	R-330Zh "Zhitel", RB-341B "Leer-3", RB-301B "Borisoglebsk-2", R-381T "Taran", R-934UM, and PSNR-8 Kredo-M1 monitoring stations
	Other nonlethal equipment	Helmets and body armor; night-vision equipment; laptops and personal communication equipment; medical supplies
Cyber warfare	Battlefield cyberattacks	Attacks targeted AFU C2 centers, soldier cell phones/mobile communication apps, AFU equipment produced by Russian military-industrial complex (like radios)
	Infrastructure cyberattacks	Attacks targeted full spectrum of government agencies, entities, critical infrastructure such as electricity grids, pipelines, railway, port, airports, etc.; banking and financial institutions; and a variety of other personal computers and private-sector business interests for political ends
Direct financial support	Russian government funds	Unknown levels; probably less than 1% of Russian gross domestic product
	Looted Ukrainian assets	Unknown levels; billions looted from Kyiv coffers in 2014
	Private oligarchs	Unknown levels; likely hundreds of millions

Table 5.1—Continued

Category	Subcategory	Summarized Levels of External Russian Support
Information warfare	n/a	Initial Novorossiya campaign superseded by pro-federalism campaign aimed domestically and internationally
Diplomatic/ political capital	n/a	Issuing passports, granting dual citizenship, recognizing DNR/LNR embassies, issuing new currency, nationalizing Donbas industries, attempting to change Ukrainian constitution, interfering in Ukrainian national elections, dominating Minsk peace framework discussions

SOURCES: RAND Arroyo Center analysis; Adam Cech and Jakub Janda, "Caught in the Act: Proof of Russian Military Intervention in Ukraine," Wilfried Martens Centre for European Studies, July 2015; Joseph Trevithick, "This Tank Has Become an Icon of Russia's Secret War in Ukraine," *War Is Boring*, June 7, 2016; Veli-Pekka Kivimaki, "Tankspotting: How to Identify the T072B3," *Bellingcat*, May 28, 2015; Maksymilian Czuperski, John Herbst, Eliot Higgins, Alina Polyakova, and Damon Wilson, "Hiding in Plain Sight: Russia's War in Ukraine," The Atlantic Council, October 15, 2015; Jonathan Ferguson and N. R. Jenzen-Jones, *Raising Red Flags: An Examination of Arms & Munitions in the Ongoing Conflict in Ukraine, 2014*, Australia: Armament Research Services (ARES), November 18, 2014; James Rupert, "Thousands of Russian Troops in Airport Push," *Newsweek*, January 23, 2015, Kofman et al., 2017; Umer Khan, "'New Generation Urban Battlespace': The Development of Russian Military Thinking and Capabilities in Urban Warfare Since the Cold War, 1991–2019," Ph.D. dissertation, University of Buckingham, January 2020; Sergey Sukhankin, "Russian Electronic Warfare in Ukraine: Between Real and Imaginable," *Eurasian Daily Monitor*, Jamestown Foundation, May 26, 2017; Oriana Pawlyk, "Sanctions Are Impacting Russia's Electronic Warfare Campaign in Ukraine, Officials Claim," Military.com, October 30, 2019; Michael Sheldon, "Russian GPS-Jamming Systems Return to Ukraine," Atlantic Council's Digital Forensic Research Lab, May 23, 2019; Tor Bukkvoll, "Russian Special Operations Forces in Crimea and Donbas," *Parameters*, Vol. 46, No. 2, Summer 2016; Nataliya Bugayova, Mason Clark, and George Barros, "Putin Accelerates Ukraine Campaign Amid Converging Crises," *Russia in Review*, March 24, 2020; Shandra and Seely, 2019; Holcomb, 2017.

First and foremost, from at least as early as mid-March 2014 (i.e., a full month before the eruption of full-scale violence), Russia began covertly providing manpower for a spectrum of activities—including training, advising, ISR-targeting and intelligence-gathering, logistical support, and eventually, combat from four broad sources:

1. Russian special forces, including personnel from all seven Spetsnaz (special assignment) GRU brigades, the Russian Airborne Forces (VDV) 45th Brigade, and the Federal Security Service[22]

2. Russian regular units, including at peak some 4,000–9,000 estimated troops during the period of conventional escalation beginning with the Russian encirclement of Ilovaisk in August 2014 through the key battles to seize Donetsk airport and the Debaltseve railway hub and affect the AFU's retreat from the border region in January–February 2015.[23]

3. PMCs, including the "notorious" Wagner Group, whose strength grew from an estimated 100 personnel to some 5,000 troops in Ukraine.[24]

4. Paramilitary "volunteers" (dobrovotsi), including thousands of veterans of the conflicts in Chechnya, Dagestan, Abkhazia, South Ossetia, and Moldova, as well as fighters from "radical groups from Russia and the former Soviet Union, including Cossack bands,

---

[22] These Russian special operators, who were typically dressed and equipped to resemble local military and police forces, served as "one of the main tools" used by the Kremlin "in initiating parts of the anti-Kiev rebellion in Donbas." By the summer of 2014, these Spetsnaz-GRU units were reportedly "engaged in the full spectrum of regular SOF tasks," including jointly planning and/or conducting some acts of sabotage, mine-laying, and hit-and-run attacks in rear areas of operations against resupply and transport lines of communication (Bukkvoll, 2016, pp. 14–19).

[23] During this period, Russian train, advise, and equip efforts appear to have refocused on transforming and consolidating the constellation of VNSAs into a conventional fighting force—rather than a guerrilla insurgency. Since then, Russia has maintained a "quick reaction force" capability to deploy as needed. Recently, Ukraine has estimated that some 3,600–4,200 Russian troops remained in Donbas (Ministry of Foreign Affairs of Ukraine, "10 Facts You Should Know About Russian Military Aggression Against Ukraine," December 19, 2019; Kofman et al., 2017, pp. 44–45; Holcomb, 2017, pp. 9–10; Rupert, 2015).

[24] PMCs like Wagner have provided supplemental manpower for a diverse range of activities "from frontal attacks on Ukrainian forces and urban fighting to intelligence gathering, information-psychological operations and sabotage/subversive operations against local actors, showcasing growing independence" (Sergey Sukhankin, "Unleashing the PMCs and Irregulars in Ukraine: Crimea and Donbas," Jamestown Foundation, September 3, 2019).

Russian Orthodox Christian radicals, Russian nationalists, and communists."[25]

Notably, in the area of manpower, from the start of the conflict, C2 structures became dominated "on both tactical and strategic levels by Russian military staff."[26]

Second, while some rebel equipment and arms were seized from Ukrainian government caches at the start of the conflict, Russia has been the primary source of lethal weaponry to the separatists, from small arms to tanks and advanced missile systems.[27] Owing to Kyiv's inability to control the Russian-Ukrainian border, Russia retained "unfettered access to supply its proxy forces with ammunition and manpower," crossing the border "at will" often in supply trucks masked as humanitarian convoys.[28] Beginning as early as June 2014, Moscow began supplying its proxy forces with heavy armored and mechanized equipment; in particular, open-source documentation of modern tanks on the battlefield widely removed any remaining doubts of Russian direct involvement.[29] Also from the earliest months of the insurgency, they received advanced short-range air-defense weaponry and heavy antiaircraft artillery pieces and munitions. As the proxy war transitioned into a conventional standoff in June–August 2014, more-advanced

---

[25] These irregular forces were encouraged by Russian state propaganda to supplement indigenous VNSAs beginning in the spring of 2014 (Holcomb, 2017, pp. 9–10; Sukhankin, 2019; International Crisis Group, 2019, p. 4).

[26] In fact, the Kremlin repeatedly purged the leadership ranks of the DNR and LNR, and many of the key heads of the DNR and LNR were "Kremlin-approved" Russian citizens or former military/intelligence officers (Shandra and Seely, 2019, pp. 26–27; Holcomb, 2017, pp. 9–10; Gianluca Mezzofiore, "Igor Strelkov: I Started War in Eastern Ukraine," *International Business Times*, November 21, 2014; Gabriela Baczynska and Aleksandar Vasovik, "Pushing Locals Aside, Russians Take Top Rebel Posts in East Ukraine," Reuters, July 27, 2014).

[27] Cech and Janda, 2015; Ferguson and Jenzen-Jones, 2014; Czuperski et al., 2015, p. 8; Trevithick, 2016; Mary Ellen Connell and Ryan Evans, "Russia's Ambiguous Warfare and Implications for the U.S. Marine Corps," *MCU Journal*, Vol. 7, No. 1, Spring 2016.

[28] Holcomb, 2017, p. 9; Czuperski et al., 2015, p. 3; Connell and Evans, 2016, pp. 30–31; "'Maskirovka' Is Russian Secret War: Sneaky Tactics Are an Old Russian Tradition," *War Is Boring*, August 26, 2014.

[29] Trevithick, 2016; Kivimaki, 2015.

munitions, medium-range air-defense systems, and larger-caliber mortar batteries were also introduced with increasing lethality.[30] Indeed, by the end of Russia's major conventional ground operations in February 2015, Moscow had reportedly "transferred more than 1,000 pieces of Russian military equipment into Ukraine including tanks, armored personnel carriers [APCs], heavy artillery pieces, and other military vehicles."[31] In the area of artillery fires, Russian forces also supported their proxies with massive cross-border shelling operations.[32]

Third, the Russian government supplied a wide variety of sophisticated, nonlethal equipment and materiel, such as night-vision equipment; drones; APCs; mobile radar systems; medical supplies; helmets and body armor; laptops and personal communication equipment; and a multitude of military trucks and special-purpose vehicles, such as mobile armored C2 centers.[33] Much of this nonlethal materiel has "shown a technological edge" and evidently been "close to NATO standards."[34] As a subcategory in the area of nonlethal materiel, we note that Russia also employed advanced EW capabilities, "such as advanced spectrum analyzers to measure signal magnitude, as well as receivers to spot audio or electrical signals," enabling VNSAs in Donbas to jam and intercept Ukrainian military radio frequencies, smartphone and cell phone signals, national communications networks, drone GPS navigation systems, and counterartillery radar batteries and satellites.[35]

---

[30] Kofman et al., 2017, p. 42; Sébastien Roblin, "The Largest-Caliber Mortar System in the World Is Shelling Cities in Syria and Ukraine," *Offiziere.ch*, April 25, 2016a; "MH17 Missile 'Came from Russia,' Dutch-Led Investigators Say," BBC News, September 28, 2016.

[31] Trevithick, 2016.

[32] Sean Case and Klement Anders, "Putin's Undeclared War: Summer 2014 Russian Artillery Strikes Against Ukraine," *Bellingcat*, December 21, 2016, pp. 2–4, 32–34; Karen DeYoung, "U.S. Releases Images It Says Show Russia Has Fired Artillery Over Border into Ukraine," *Washington Post*, July 27, 2014.

[33] Cech and Janda, 2015, pp. 3–19; Czuperski et al., 2015, pp. 8–10; Rupert, 2015; Kofman et al., 2017, p. 44.

[34] Khan, 2020, p. 62.

[35] Indeed, according to Ukrainian officials, in the first three years of the insurgency, the Kremlin provided its proxy forces at least some "43 pieces of modern EW equip-

Fourth, in the cyber warfare domain, the proxy war in Donbas became a "scorched-earth testing ground" for Russian tactics.[36] Shortly after Yanukovych's ouster, separatist sympathizers, including Russian government agents, began launching mass cyberattacks on government and parliamentary websites, as well as critical infrastructure, such as electrical distribution networks, media outlets, railway firms, and ports.[37] Most infamously, in June 2017, Russian military hackers known as "Sandworm" orchestrated an attack on Ukrainian cyber infrastructure with the NotPetya malware, causing an estimated $10 billion in damages, "[eating] Ukraine's computers alive" and gravely disrupting the operations of most government agencies.[38] As discussed in more detail below, these attacks also targeted apps and electronics on the battlefield.

Fifth, relatedly, the Kremlin orchestrated information operations on a mass scale in support of VNSA agendas. Many of these initiatives conformed to the KGB-era playbook to use "active measures," while other elements of Russian doctrine in Donbas were evidently more novel.[39] Because much excellent work has been done on this topic since 2014,[40] here we simply note that the Kremlin's information warfare campaign was initially designed to weaponize the concept of Novorossiya ("New Russia"), a political-ideological rallying cry for the separatists invoking historical times

---

ment" (Sheldon, 2019; Sukhankin, 2017; Kagan et al., 2019, p. 36; Pawlyk, 2019; Connell and Evans, 2016, p. 38).

[36] Andy Greenberg, "The Untold Story of NotPetya, the Most Destructive Cyberattack in History," *Wired*, August 22, 2018; Kagan, Bugayova, and Cafarella, June 2019, p. 14; Kofman et al. 2017, pp. 50–55.

[37] Sukhankin, 2017; Greenberg, 2018; U.S. Department of State, 2020.

[38] Greenberg, 2019; Kagan, Bugayova, and Cafarella, June 2019, p. 14.

[39] Kagan et al., 2019, p. 34.

[40] See, for instance, Keir Giles, "Handbook of Russian Information Warfare," Research Division, NATO Defense College, November 2016; Jolanta Darczewska, *The Anatomy of Russian Information Warfare, the Crimean Operation, a Case Study*, Warsaw, Poland: Centre for Eastern Studies, May 2014; Mark Galeotti, "The 'Gerasimov Doctrine' and Russian Non-Linear War," *In Moscow's Shadows*, July 6, 2014; and Mark Galeotti, "The Mythical 'Gerasimov Doctrine' and the Language of Threat," *Critical Studies on Security*, Vol. 7, No. 2, 2019, pp. 157–161.

when Ukraine was part of the Russian empire.[41] However, this "signature narrative" ultimately resulted in a "campaign that lacked ideological cohesion commonly found in grassroots movements," and the Kremlin abandoned its "effort to create an image of public support" for this ambitious project "intended to incorporate the whole of South and Eastern Ukraine."[42] Instead, after the project's failure, Moscow's information campaign refocused on "organiz[ing] and fund[ing] a pan-Ukrainian campaign for a 'soft federalisation' of the country . . . [and] creat[ing] an illusion of widespread support for these activities."[43]

Sixth, Russian secret services also provided VNSAs in Donbas with a considerable amount of cash. At their inceptions in 2014, the DNR and LNR governments decided not to collect taxes until military operations had ended, at which point Moscow evidently came to bankroll the new statelets.[44] These illicit funds allegedly flowed to separatist leaders from three main sources: (1) Kremlin coffers, including via Ministry of Defense wire transfers and Federal Security Service couriers "carrying suitcases stuffed with several million dollars"; (2) Ukrainian government accounts and assets looted by Yanukovych and his political allies in 2014 to the tune of "tens of billions of dollars," which were subsequently funneled back to separatists at a rate of tens of millions weekly; and (3) Russian oligarchs and private businessmen.[45]

Finally, Moscow expended significant diplomatic and political capital to increase the legitimacy of the DNR and LNR breakaway regions, including

---

[41] Kofman et al., 2017, p. 36; International Crisis Group, 2019, pp. 2–3.

[42] Shandra and Seely, 2019, pp. 30–31; Holcomb, 2017, p. 8; Mikhail Suslov, "The Production of 'Novorossiya': A Territorial Brand in Public Debates," *Europe-Asia Studies*, Vol. 69, No. 2, 2017.

[43] Shandra and Seely, 2019, p. vii, pp. 36–37.

[44] Indeed, tranches of leaked emails by Russian officials apparently confirm that the DNR and the LNR administrative structures (i.e., "governments") "only remained solvent and continued to function due to Russian funding." They also suggest that the Kremlin has "micromanaged" the financial and economic policymaking of the DNR/LNR proxy regimes (Shandra and Seely, 2019, pp. 32–34).

[45] Oleg Shynkareno, "Who's Funding East Ukraine Militancy?" Institute for War and Peace, May 16, 2014; Kofman et al., 2017, pp. 59–60; International Crisis Group, 2019, p. 4.

by "recognizing passports and other legal documents issued by separatist authorities, attempting to establish 'embassies' for its proxy forces across Europe, switching the currency of separatist regions from the Ukrainian hryvnia to the Russian ruble, and allowing its proxies to 'nationalize' industries in their territory by forcibly seizing control of them."[46] Moscow also increased efforts to "grant Russian citizenship to Ukrainians to increase leverage."[47] Meanwhile, transcending audiences in Donbas, Moscow has attempted to supply political support and legitimacy to its proxies through subversive actions, such as attempts to change Ukraine's constitution and aggressive interference in Ukrainian democratic elections.[48]

Tactical and Operational Military Challenges to Ukraine (2014–2020)

At the tactical and operational levels, Russian proxy support to VNSAs in Donbas increased their lethality and posed at least six serious challenges to what otherwise should have been Ukrainian conventional superiority in the domains of manpower, air power, artillery fires, armored infantry maneuvers, and ISR/information/cyber/electronic warfare operations.

First, Moscow's provision of short-range air-defense weaponry was effective at neutralizing the Ukrainian military's air superiority. Indeed, from the opening battles of April–May 2014, the rebels successfully downed both rotary- and fixed-wing PSU aircraft using Russian-supplied surface-to-air missiles (SAMs) and man-portable air-defense systems, and "by mid-August, Ukraine had lost so much tactical and transport aviation that its air force was unable to participate in the conflict."[49] Thus, by the time the proxy war escalated to conventional warfare, Russia and its proxies had "effectively gained control of the skies" and nullified the PSU's ability to provide CAS and airlift; during subsequent conventional fighting between August 2014

---

[46] Holcomb, 2017, p. 11.

[47] Bugayova, Clark, and Barros, 2020.

[48] Shandra and Seely, July 2019, p. vii, 36–37.

[49] Kofman et al., 2017, pp. 42–44.

and February 2015, proxies using Russian air defense systems destroyed 19 additional PSU aircraft, further degrading Ukraine's ability even to defend its own airspace.[50] Further confounding Kyiv, Russian proxies have also successfully employed advanced EW technologies (discussed in detail below) "to keep the Ukrainian air force at bay" and drones to spot artillery barrages.[51] Although Ukraine has made some gradual strides in rebuilding its air forces in the years since the Russian invasion, the PSU's attack helicopters and CAS capabilities remain effectively neutralized because of a lack of "sophisticated electronic countermeasures and air defense suppression capabilities."[52]

Second, provision of advanced tanks, along with supporting artillery fires, discussed separately below, have created multiple challenges across a "dispersed battlefield," forcing AFU forces to refrain from entering the thin stretch of "no-man's land" between frontline forces, and rendering close combat urban warfare all but impossible in the fortified cities of the DNR and the LNR.[53] Russian tanks proved "decisive" in the separatists' early key victories in February–March 2014, such as capturing the strategic town of Debaltseve, and again in August 2014–February 2015 during watershed battles at Ilovaisk and the Donetsk and Luhansk airports.[54] In short, Moscow's provision of tanks and advanced munitions "were particularly effective tactics on the ground to intimidate and subdue local populations as well

---

[50] Jane's/IHS, "Ukraine: Air Force," updated July 5, 2019.

[51] Niklas Masuhr, "Lessons of the War in Ukraine for Western Military Strategy," *CSS Analyses in Security Policy*, No. 242, April 2019, p. 2; Khan, 2020, p. 78.

[52] Connell and Evans, 2016, p. 38.

[53] As Holcomb observes, while the AFU has generally "demonstrated itself to be superior to the irregular forces facing them in Eastern Ukraine," it remains "vulnerable to the massed armored units and heavy artillery of the Russian Armed Forces" (Holcomb, 2017, p. 14).

[54] Viacheslav Shramovych, "Ukraine's Deadliest Day: The Battle of Ilovaisk, August 2014," BBC Ukrainian, August 29, 2019; "The Battle of Ilovaisk: Mapping Russian Military Presence in Eastern Ukraine, August–September 2014," *Forensic Architecture Project*, undated; Maria Tscetkova and Aleksandar Vasovic, "Exclusive: Charred Tanks in Ukraine Point to Russian Involvement," Reuters, October 23, 2014; Tom Parfitt, "Russian Tanks, Troops 'Decisive in Eastern Ukraine Battles,'" *Chicagorazom*, March 31, 2015.

as counter Ukrainian national defense forces," as evidenced by the priority set by Kyiv to acquire Javelin antitank missiles from Washington, which became a "game-changer" when first provided in 2018 by finally "forcing Russian tanks to back off."[55] By way of tactical and operational adaptation since then, AFU forces "seem to be testing Russian resolve and commitment by using the so-called 'creeping advances' tactic" in the "no-man's land that divides government forces from Russian-backed separatists"; between 2017 and 2020, this tactic resulted in the AFU slowly pushing "about 9 km deeper" into separatist-controlled territory.[56]

Third, in conjunction with heavy armored weaponry, Russian artillery often proved decisive in halting Ukrainian government ground offensives. In particular, Russian investments in indirect fires and counterbattery radar provided decisive tactical advantages in Donbas in terms of "fire-power/range" and "providing maximum responsiveness when windows of opportunity present themselves on the dynamic multidomain battlefield."[57] For instance, during critical junctures early in the war, use of heavy artillery from firing positions inside Russia proved vital in helping separatists retake strategic positions inside Ukraine (such as the Savur-Mohyla heights and Marynivka-Kuybyshevo border crossing area) and disrupt enemy supply lines.[58] As the case in point: With the separatists facing an early defeat and the AFU preparing to make a "final push to the border to cut off the supply lines of the paramilitary forces from the Russian sponsors," on July 11, 2014, a massive, coordinated, combined cross-border barrage on Ukraine's 24th and 72nd Mechanized Brigades assembled near the town of Zelenopillya wiped out the two battalions in two to three minutes, demoralizing govern-

---

[55] Howard Altman, "Lessons for the US Military from the Russian Invasion of Ukraine," *Military Times*, March 6, 2020; John Vandiver, "Pentagon to Send More Arms and Equipment to Ukraine," *Stars and Stripes*, June 19, 2019.

[56] Balazs Jarabik, "Escalation in Donbas: Ukraine Fights for the Status Quo," *War on the Rocks*, February 8, 2017; Christopher Miller, "Anxious Ukraine Risks Escalation in 'Creeping Offensive,'" Radio Free Europe–Radio Liberty, January 30, 2017; Jane's/IHS, "Ukraine: Army," last updated February 12, 2020.

[57] Liam Collins and Harrison Morgan, "King of Battle: Russia Breaks Out the Big Guns," Association of the United States Army, January 22, 2019.

[58] Case and Anders, undated, pp. 33, 38–39.

ment forces and marking the end of "the high-water mark for the Ukrainian offensive."[59] As discussed in more detail below, the sophisticated artillery attack was facilitated by a coordinated swarm of targeting drones and a simultaneous cyber-attack on Ukrainian command, control, and communications structures, illustrating how Russia has pioneered proxy warfare by integrating UAV networks with "forward observers and fire direction centers" to achieve near-real-time targeting advantages.[60] Similarly, during the intense battles to control Luhansk and Donetsk airports in 2014, the "devastating results" of Russian long-range standoff heavy artillery and mortars "mimic[ed] the effects of close-air support."[61] Indeed, Russian-supplied artillery caused an estimated 80 percent of casualties in Eastern Ukraine in 2014, and by the end of Russia's second major offensive in February 2015, the AFU had "lost two-thirds of its armored vehicles to Russian tanks, artillery, and rockets."[62] Critically, because of Russian proxy support in these areas, the AFU was likewise forced to adapt by relying heavily on its artillery fires during these battles (versus classic population-centric counterinsurgency operations), "a blunt weapon that has wreaked havoc on civilian areas in separatist-held territory and is thought to account for 80% of separatist casualties."[63] As noted below, civilian casualties resulting from Ukraine's forced reliance on tanks and other heavy artillery and weaponry have had both important tactical/operational-level and strategic-level effects by "alienat[ing] the local population of Donbas region from the Ukrainian government and has increased their support for the Russian proxy forces and the separatists."[64]

---

[59] Collins and Morgan, 2019; Khan, 2020, p. 72.

[60] Connell and Evans, 2016, p. 43; Collins and Morgan, 2019; Khan, 2020, pp. 73, 79.

[61] Collins and Morgan, 2019; Khan, 2020, pp. 72, 90–91.

[62] By another recent estimate, Moscow and its proxy forces have destroyed at least 150 Ukrainian MBTs in the DNR and the LNR since 2014 (Collins and Morgan, 2019; Connell and Evans, 2016, p. 38; Oren Dorell, "Analysis: Ukraine Forces Outmanned, Outgunned by Rebels," USA Today, February 23, 2015; Masuhr, 2019, p. 2; Jane's, February 12, 2020).

[63] Dorell, 2015.

[64] Khan, 2020, pp. 67–68.

Fourth, Russian introduction of novel EW technologies confounded Ukrainian tactics and operations and delivered blows to the AFU's critical electronic infrastructure, achieving "kinetic effects" by disrupting C2 networks, air defenses, ISR collection, and weapons targeting by jamming or "spoofing" radio signals, radar systems, and GPS tracking.[65] Moscow's "impressive" technological edges in the employment of EW technologies have included counter–unmanned aircraft system (counter-UAS) tactics, such as utilizing "high power microwave systems to jam or bring down enemy drones," which between 2015 and 2017 resulted in the downing of some 100 Ukrainian drones.[66] Russia's pioneering EW efforts have also been utilized, for instance, to activate the "radio proximity fuses of incoming munitions prematurely to defend friendly forces against artillery, rocket and missile attacks" and to hijack "direction-finding systems in addition to jammers to zero in on Ukrainian positions and launch artillery strikes on those locations."[67] As another example of proxy warfare EW innovation, in 2015, Moscow "engage[d] in mass sabotage of Russian-made radios that Ukraine was using at the time by triggering some sort of kill switch, which [Ukrainian officials] described as a 'virus,' remotely . . . [raising] questions about what sort of failsafe devices Russia may be hiding inside the military equipment it sells to partners around the world."[68] Forced to adapt, the AFU resorted to "much more vulnerable commercial radios and cellular networks, which the Russians then also relentlessly attacked."[69]

Fifth, the Ukraine case demonstrates new tactical- and operational-level challenges posed by the marriage of state-sponsored cyberwar and proxy warfare. Indeed, the persistence of Russian meddling in Eastern Ukraine increased the "risk of disruptive cyber-attacks, including against critical

---

[65] Sukhankin, 2017; Joseph Trevithick, "Ukrainian Officer Details Russian Electronic Warfare Tactics Including Radio 'Virus,'" *The Drive*, October 30, 2019b; Joseph Trevithick, "Russian GPS-Jamming Systems Return to Ukraine," *The Medium*, May 23, 2019a.

[66] Trevithick, 2019a; Khan, 2020, p. 62, 81.

[67] Russia has also used UAVs "with electro-optical cameras and electronic direction finders to locate and then jam counter-battery radars ahead of mortar and other artillery strikes" (Khan, 2020, p. 62; Trevithick, 2019a).

[68] Trevithick, 2019a.

[69] Trevithick, 2019a.

national infrastructure, such as energy grids, water supply, metro systems, ports and airports mostly executed by groups associated with Russia."[70] For instance, describing the damage caused by the devastating June 2017 NotPetya malware attack, Ukrainian minister of infrastructure Volodymyr Omelyan succinctly stated, "The government was dead."[71] Furthermore, Russian cyberattacks also often affected tactics and operations on the battle-field directly, including targeting of applications on mobile Android devices used by Ukrainian artillery units, which from late 2014 through December 2016 reportedly allowed hackers associated with the GRU to monitor com-munications between AFU forces and track and target their movements.[72]

Sixth, sophisticated nonlethal equipment and materiel have also report-edly confounded the AFU on the tactical and operational levels in a myriad of ways. For instance, the tactical effect of Russian-supplied body armor and body armor–piercing ammunition in Eastern Ukraine has been to "over-whelm normal infantry, especially when delivered with night vision and snipers."[73] More generally, while close combat urban warfare situations have been relatively rare in this case, Moscow's proxies in Donbas, having appar-ently learned from the Russian experience in Chechnya, "displayed innova-tive tactics" in sometimes using "serpentine" networks of tunnels, sewers, bunkers, and underground communications systems to stymie superior Ukrainian/NATO ISR targeting technologies.[74]

Finally, we caveat that despite these massive levels of advanced support, separatists in the DNR and the LNR would still not have been able to fend off the AFU without direct manpower provided by Moscow. For instance, the injection of professional Russian troops, particularly the decision to operate largely through PMCs, such as Wagner Group, had important C2 implications for VNSA efforts.[75] They reportedly demonstrated a relatively

[70] Jane's/IHS, "Ukraine: Executive Summary," updated March 23, 2020.

[71] Greenberg, 2019.

[72] Mohan Gazula, "Cyber Warfare Conflict Analysis and Case Studies," Massachusetts Institute of Technology, Working Paper CISL# 2017-10, May 2017, pp. 61–62.

[73] Connell and Evans, 2016, p. 38.

[74] Khan, 2020, p. 91.

[75] Sukhankin, 2019.

high level of military professionalism and competence, albeit less than that of the "highly skilled special forces elements supported them in the battle area and in the rear of the Ukrainian forces."[76] Importantly, by also deploying tens of thousands of conventional deterrent forces in the rear of operations, Moscow "provide[d] separatist structures with security guarantees against superior formations of the Armed Force of Ukraine, allowing them to deploy combat-ready troops forward and conduct tactical offensive operations without engaging in serious efforts to develop defensive depth . . . [and] without needing to plan against major counter-offensive operations [after August 2014]."[77] In short, external personnel support was required to make these proxies sufficiently capable so that Russia could continue to operate with some degree of (im)plausible deniability rather than engaging in a large-scale direct invasion. However, these proxies by themselves could likely not have survived without professional external troops on the ground.

Strategic Military Challenges to Ukraine (2014–2020)

In the Ukraine case study, the implications of external support to VNSAs may be more relevant at the strategic level than at the tactical/operational levels. Indeed, even with massive Russian support, Moscow's proxy forces have yet to win any major tactical/operational battlefield victories against the AFU without direct combat support from thousands of conventional troops, as the conflict stalemated after early 2015.[78] At least five implications emerge as particularly important at the strategic level in this case.

First, while some degree of Russian involvement was evident from the start, the Kremlin's obfuscation, active measures, and other covert tactics described above allowed it to slow the response of the international community and avoid eliciting a direct military response by the United States or its European allies. This was an example of a "'norm-setting' intervention

---

[76] Kagan et al., 2019, p. 36; Sukhankin, 2019.

[77] Holcomb, 2017, p. 9.

[78] Holcomb, 2017, pp. 10–11.

strategy" intended to exploit against the West its own "rules of the game" by "[framing] the conflict as a self-determination crisis within Ukraine as opposed to Russia objecting to Ukraine's closer association with the EU and NATO,"[79] At the same time, maintaining deniability through employment of political warfare tactics may have produced disproportionate "golden hour" gains by emphasizing greater investments "early in the enemy's campaign of street protests, agitation, and subversion" versus "the later campaign of open warfare"; however, as the Ukraine experience also reflects, recognizing the "often hard to detect" initial phases of proxy-war campaigns may become much easier in the future because of broader trends in social media, forensic geotagging, etc.[80] Indeed, as plausible deniability declined over time, Russian active measures ultimately failed to build to a critical mass and create an "ideological cohesion commonly found in grassroots movements," thus forcing Moscow to moderate its end goals for Donbas from full annexation to greater political autonomy/federalism.[81] Importantly for the study of future proxy warfare, this case study thus highlights the limits of maintaining deniability while building an artificially invoked proxy resistance movement, as opposed to working through an ideologically committed, preexisting indigenous insurgent group.

Second, on a strategic-military level, before its invasion in 2022, Russia's proxy warfare efforts arguably slowed Ukraine's formal westward drift, at least in terms of formal relations with NATO. Indeed, historically, NATO has been reluctant to consider membership bids of applicants with ongoing territorial disputes with neighbors (e.g., Cyprus). To these ends, some have suggested that a proxy war stalemate in the breakaway regions in Ukraine (like in Georgia) could provide Moscow a "de-facto veto" over its neigh-

---

[79] Christopher Borgen, "Law, Rhetoric, Strategy: Russia and Self-Determination Before and After Crimea," *International Law Studies*, Vol. 91, No. 216, 2015, pp. 265–267; Eileen Babbitt, "Self-Determination as a Component of Conflict Intractability: Implications for Negotiation," in Hurst Hannum and Eileen Babbit, eds., *Negotiating Self-Determination*, 2006, pp. 115–118.

[80] Connell and Evans, 2016, p. 42.

[81] Holcomb, 2017, p. 8.

bor's destiny in NATO.[82] At least so long as the conflict remains unresolved, NATO members will likely remain wary of Ukraine's candidacy because as a permanent member it would enjoy Article 5 security guarantees; under such mutual defense treaty obligations, an escalation of instability or another Russian invasion could compel a direct U.S./NATO military response, including even triggering an overt confrontation between Washington/ Brussels and Moscow. In short, this case study underlines Russia's willingness to use force to block a country in its near abroad from fully integrating into Western institutions. This, in turn, has soured Western interest in these ultimate goals, a modern application of Soviet-era "reflexive control" strategy—i.e., "goals set by the Kremlin that serve its own interests, yet that Ukraine and the West also pursue."[83] At the same time, perhaps paradoxically, Russian proxy aggression deepened cooperation between Ukraine and the West on security and economic matters as the United States, EU, and NATO have tried to stabilize Ukraine in the face of Russian interference. In particular, Western-Ukrainian military ties have deepened significantly through increased combined exercises and training efforts since 2014 and have accelerated Kyiv's "ambitious reform effort designed to modernize the AFU and meet NATO standards by 2020."[84]

Third, as noted above, relatively high civilian casualties inflicted by AFU's forced reliance on blunt tactics (i.e., employing heavy unit and artillery) have also had strategic-level effects by alienating the local population, in breach of a classic, population-centric counterinsurgency strategy. Nevertheless, in this case study, the net strategic implications of casualty sensitivity on public opinion and sustaining domestic political support have been ambiguous, with no clear winner on either side. Indeed, despite casualties from indiscriminate AFU shelling, "The popular mood in areas of eastern

---

[82] John Deni, "Tie Lethal Aid for Ukraine to an Admission That NATO Made a Mistake," *War on the Rocks*, December 22, 2017; Jonathan Brunson, "Implementing the Minsk Agreements Might Drive Ukraine to Civil War. That's Been Russia's Plan All Along," *War on the Rocks*, February 1, 2019.

[83] Brunson, 2019. On Russia's "reflexive control" tendencies, see Annie Kowalewski, "Disinformation and Reflexive Control: The New Cold War," *Georgetown Security Studies Review*, February 1, 2017.

[84] Holcomb, 2017, p. 10.

Ukraine outside Kyiv's control appears ambivalent about the region's political future. What emerges from (admittedly limited) poll and interviews is that the conflict has left people both alienated from Kyiv and disappointed with Moscow. Locals are tired of the war and appear ready to side with anyone who offers a plausible plan for fixing infrastructure, supplying aid and resolving the question of the region's political status."[85]

Fourth, as discussed in detail above, Ukrainian leadership quickly learned the escalatory risks of inducing greater Russian involvement when its offensives threatened victory; though Moscow clearly sought to avoid a direct invasion similar to Crimea, it ultimately found such escalation unavoidable. Subsequently, Kyiv's military strategy was forced to adapt, embracing an "erode and probe" and later a "creeping offensive" strategic approach to gradually deplete VNSA forces and resources without triggering a Russian counteroffensive, as occurred in the summer of 2014. For instance, as another recent International Crisis Group report explains, "Front-line [Ukrainian] commanders are more confident than in the past that their troops could make serious inroads into separatist territory, or even destroy the entities, but the main factor stopping such an attempt is threat of another major Russian invasion."[86] Of course, this also implies that, because Kyiv believes that it could defeat the insurgency in the absence of Russian aid, were Moscow to become distracted (for instance, by a major economic or domestic political crisis), Ukraine might seize on the window of opportunity to seek a military solution rather than completing the path

---

[85] Similarly, in a "rare" 2016 public opinion poll in the DNR and the LNR, only 44 percent of the population supported joining Russia, while more than half (55 percent) favored remaining in Ukraine (of which, this share split 35 percent versus 20 percent supporting regional autonomy versus no autonomy; International Crisis Group, 2019, p. 14).

[86] International Crisis Group, "Ukraine: The Line," Briefing No. 81, July 18, 2016. As a more recent International Crisis Group report concluded, "For [new President Volodymyr Zelenskyy], the worst option of course would be to try to forcibly retake the territories, as an all-out offensive would likely provoke a military response from Moscow and a bloodbath in Donbas. It could even lead Moscow, according to a former Kremlin official, to recognize the statelets' independence, much as it did in 2008 during its war with Georgia over the breakaway republics of Abkhazia and South Ossetia" (International Crisis Group, 2019, p. 17).

of political reconciliation begun by the Minsk agreements.[87] On the other hand, Kyiv is aware that it would risk losing the support of its Western allies if it seized such an opportunity to launch an offensive; indeed, such concerns over escalation delayed provision of U.S. lethal aid to the government until April 2018, the fourth year of the proxy war.

Conclusion: Effects of Russian Proxy Warfare in Donbas

Russian support between 2014 and 2020 was absolutely essential to help separatist movements carve out autonomous zones in the Donbas region. Russian state personnel and contractors trained and organized separatist forces. At the time the research for this case study was conducted (2020), Russian operatives were—and had been for some time—extensively embedded throughout all echelons of the separatist forces. Russia provided sophisticated military equipment, including main battle tanks and short-range air-defense weaponry. Without Russian support, these forces would have almost certainly collapsed. At the same time, this case study illustrates that even extensive state support alone is insufficient to build a highly effective insurgency against relatively capable militaries; without broad-based local support, the Donbas separatists remained limited in their military potential even years after the inception of the conflict. Were Russian military support to cease, analysts argued in 2019, the AFU would easily "regain control over the Russian-occupied territories."[88]

On the other hand, Russia did not need to build a highly effective hybrid force to achieve some of its strategic goals; it needed only to develop a force that was sufficiently effective that it could limit its direct military involvement. Russian proxy warfare succeeded in destabilizing the country and giving Russia some leverage over Ukrainian government foreign and security policy at relatively low cost to Russia. Ultimately, however, Russia determined that such leverage was inadequate to realize its strategic objectives, leading to its invasion in 2022.

---

[87] Brunson, 2019.

[88] Kagan et al., 2019, p. 36.

CHAPTER 6

The Houthi Rebellion: Iran and the Gulf Arabs in Yemen

Introduction

Since 2004 but especially following the Arab spring in 2011, the internationally recognized government of Yemen has fought insurgents from the Houthi movement and others allied with it. The Houthis, or Ansar Allah (the Supporters of God) as the group self-identifies, can be classified as a proxy group because they receive state support from Iran in the form of weapons, training, and financial assistance (although the level of Iranian assistance and its influence over the Houthis is considerably less than in the other case studies in this report).[1] The Houthis also possess statelike military capabilities based on their alliance with a portion of the Yemeni military that began fighting the internationally recognized Yemeni government in 2015. Those military forces use state-purchased weapons (e.g., armor, artillery, ballistic missiles) and state-provided training (e.g., C2 practices, employment of weapons) to support the Houthis and to secure their own position within Yemen. Beginning in 2015, a coalition led by Saudi Arabia entered the conflict on the side of the Yemeni government.[2]

---

[1] For an analysis that distinguishes between Iran's various proxy relationships, see Ariane M. Tabatabai, Jeffrey Martini, and Becca Wasser, *The Iran Threat Network (ITN): Four Models of Iran's Nonstate Client Partnerships*, Santa Monica, Calif.: RAND Corporation, RR-4231-A, 2021.

[2] There is a significant debate among the analytic community on the degree to which the Houthis have subordinated themselves to Iranian control, as well as a debate over the relative weight of the Houthi fighters versus the breakaway Yemeni military forces in their alliance. This research is not intended to settle those questions, nor does it

The Houthis have showed tactical proficiency since the mid-2000s but became a more sophisticated military force because of their alliance with Saleh loyalists from the Yemeni Army and the integration of weapons and new tactics, techniques, and procedures (TTPs) provided by Iran. As time went on, the group leveraged its relationships with Saleh loyalists and Iran to develop its own manufacturing and development capabilities. Today, the Houthis are one of the more capable nonstate military actors in the Middle East, and there is every reason to expect further increases in their capabilities in the coming years.

To prevent the Houthis from using ballistic missiles as terror weapons against Saudi Arabia, the United States has had to maintain and train Saudi personnel on the operation of U.S.-origin missile defense systems (in particular, Patriot batteries). In addition, the United States has deployed its own missile defense systems (both Patriot and Terminal High Altitude Area Defense) to aid in the protection of U.S. personnel operating from Saudi Arabia at such installations as Prince Sultan Airbase.[3] To maintain freedom of navigation through the Red Sea, the United States increased its presence of Carrier assets and added an Amphibious Ready Group,[4] which are designed to deter the Houthis from employing coastal missiles against maritime vessels or to respond to Houthi aggression should deterrence fail.

At the time of writing (summer 2022), the Houthis arguably were winning the conflict. At an international level, the costs of the conflict (both direct and reputational) had driven several members of the Saudi-led military coalition to cease their support for government forces. Meanwhile, the Houthis' advanced capabilities were tying up certain scarce U.S. military capabilities, such as air and missile defense assets. Although the conflict is ongoing, it has already demonstrated the ability of state-backed insurgents

---

address in depth the use of proxy forces by the United Arab Emirates (UAE) in support of the internationally recognized government (e.g., the Hadrami Elite Forces). Rather, this research focuses more narrowly on the military implications of the Houthi proxy threat for to the United States and its affected partners.

[3]   Joanne Stocker, "US to Deploy Additional Troops, Patriot Batteries and THAAD System to Saudi Arabia," *The Defense Post*, October 11, 2019.

[4]   Philip Athey, "Thousands of Marines with 26th MEU Move into the Red Sea," *Marine Corps Times*, January 13, 2020.

to pose serious challenges to even relatively well-armed and -trained militaries, such as those of Saudi Arabia.

As with the other case studies in this report, this chapter addresses three core issues. First, it documents the capabilities gained by the Houthis through foreign support that it would not otherwise have had. Second, it reveals the tactical- and operational-level military challenges that foreign support posed to external interveners, including the Saudi-led coalition and the United States. Finally, it shows how foreign support may have altered the course of the conflict at a strategic level, although such claims come with the caveat that the war has not ended. However, this case differs somewhat from the other three cases. While foreign support was critical to the Vietminh, Vietcong, and forces of the DNR and LNR, the Houthis were highly capable militarily even before Iran provided support (in part because the Houthis possessed much of the military capability of the Yemeni Army from before the collapse of the regime). As is demonstrated in this case, however, Iranian support provided the Houthis with yet more advanced capabilities. These capabilities, in turn, posed many of the same military challenges at the tactical, operational, and strategic levels that VNSAs in the prior chapters posed.

Background

The Houthi movement, named after the family and tribe of the same name that dominates its leadership, is a longtime armed actor in Yemen. Its lineage and authority rests on the role that its supporters' religious identity group (Zaydis) played in ruling North Yemen prior to unification and prior to the creation of the modern Yemeni state.[5] The Houthis are particularly strong in Saada governorate but have supporters throughout much of what was North Yemen (formally the Yemen Arab Republic). The Houthis contested the central government's control of territory in northern governorates throughout the 2000s, waging both an insurgency against the state and

---

[5] There is not a perfect overlap between the Houthi movement and the Zaydi (a branch of Shia Islam) identity group. The most general distinction is that all Houthis (members of the leading family and tribe) are Zaydis, but not all Zaydis are Houthis. Furthermore, the Houthis have aligned with many non-Zaydi groups, such as some leading Hashemite families in Yemen.

cross-border attacks on Saudi Arabia,[6] which abuts Houthi territory to the north.

The current civil war that began in 2015 is the period in which the Houthis have matured as a proxy group and developed into a greater threat to the United States and its regional partners. Specifically, the upheaval of the Arab Spring and the subsequent civil war in Yemen created two oppor-tunities for the Houthis that the group has duly exploited. The first oppor-tunity was that a fraught leadership transition from long-standing President Ali Abdullah Saleh to his successor, current President Abdu Rabbu Man-sour Hadi, created an opportunity for a Houthi challenge to the new leader-ship. President Hadi lacked broad legitimacy, did not have the full support of the Saleh loyalists he displaced, and presided over a transition in which crucial aspects of governance were up for consideration, including the scope of federalism in Yemen.[7] This created strong incentives for the Houthis, and the Saleh loyalists who wished to retain power, to challenge the new Hadi government.

Second, and directly related to the Houthis' willingness to accept for-eign state support, this context also created incentives for Iran to influence political outcomes in the region. Specifically, Iran was incentivized to back aspirants to power who would promise better relations with Iran and tie down its regional rivals (e.g., Saudi Arabia) with border challenges. On these counts, Yemen was an inviting space because the Houthis had previously engaged in border skirmishes with Saudi forces,[8] and the Houthis' ascen-dance in Yemen would distract from the resources and attention that Saudi Arabia and its partners could devote to challenging Iranian positions in the Levant. Yemen was also inviting terrain for a cost-imposition strategy, as Iran could qualitatively increase Houthi capabilities with modest invest-

---

[6] Barak Salmoni, Bryce Loidolt, and Madeleine Wells, *Regime and Periphery in Northern Yemen: The Huthi Phenomenon*, Santa Monica, Calif.: RAND Corporation, MG-962-DIA, 2010.

[7] Maysaa Shuja Al-Din, "Federalism in Yemen: A Catalyst for War, the Present Reality, and the Inevitable Future," Sanaa Center for Strategic Studies, February 2019.

[8] Christopher Boucek, "War in Saada: From Local Insurrection to National Chal-lenge," Carnegie Endowment, April 2010.

ment, while its regional opponents would be forced to pour resources into a campaign to recover the status quo ante.[9]

When the Houthis challenged the new order in 2015, the weak capabilities of the new government combined with the Houthis' alliance with Saleh loyalists enabled the Houthis to quickly overrun much of the country. Within days, Houthi-aligned forces reached the outskirts of Aden, a city that operates as the unofficial capital of southern Yemen. Aden was seen as the Hadi government's last stand, since it sits at the opposite end of the spectrum—geographically and in terms of its sectarian composition—from the Houthi stronghold of Saada. Although Hadi himself was forced to flee Yemen, Aden ultimately held. Crucial to this outcome was the assistance of the Saudi-led Coalition, which intervened with air power, and a UAE-led advise-and-assist operation. In this effort, the UAE worked through irregular forces that too can be characterized as proxies.

Although the Saudi-led Coalition initially made considerable progress in rolling back Houthi gains, the Yemeni forces they backed failed to retake the capital city (Sanaa), and the civil war settled into what appeared to be a stalemate. However, since the summer of 2019, the UAE has greatly reduced its involvement in the conflict, and Saudi Arabia, under other pressures and under much criticism for the conduct of its air campaign, has also reduced the tempo of strikes in Yemen.[10] Furthermore, the internationally recognized government, which is based on a fragile coalition of actors, has broken down into open infighting, including armed conflict. This has enabled a renewed Houthi advance that has further strengthened their position in the conflict.[11]

---

[9] Maysaa Shuja Al-Din, "Iran and Houthis: Between Political Alliances and Sectarian Tensions," *Al-Masdar Online*, June 15, 2017.

[10] Declan Walsh and David Kirkpatrick, "U.A.E. Pulls Most Forces from Yemen in Blow to Saudi War Effort," *New York Times*, July 11, 2019; Aziz El Yaakoubi, "Saudi-Led Coalition Air Strikes in Yemen Down 80%: U.N. Envoy," Reuters, November 22, 2019.

[11] Naseh Shaker, "Will Marib Province Survive Houthi Offensive After Fall of al-Jawf?" *Al Monitor*, March 13, 2020.

How State Support Enhanced Houthi Capabilities

As noted in the case background, there are really two sources of the Houthis' statelike capabilities. The first is the military equipment and experience that it inherited or seized from state military units that remained loyal to former President Saleh and joined him in his ill-fated alliance with the Houthis. Houthi fighters killed President Saleh in 2017 to preempt what they saw as his plans to "flip" and cut a deal with Saudi Arabia.[12] Not all units defected en masse, but among the units whose capabilities were largely absorbed by the Houthi-led civil war coalition were the Presidential Guard forces.[13] In addition, the Houthis overran and absorbed many of the capabilities that resided in Yemen's 1st Armored Division.[14] Elements of the Yemeni Air Force also sided with the Houthis;[15] however, their capabilities were largely reduced by the Saudi-led intervention that followed.[16] Perhaps most significantly, the Houthis seized or co-opted the military leaders who controlled much of Yemen's missile forces.[17] Analysts have speculated that the Houthis control 60 to 70 percent of the military capabilities previously resident in the country's military forces.[18] As summarized in a Chatham House study, "While the assorted forces affiliated with the Sanaa-based Ansar Allah

---

[12] "Al Houthi: The Assassination of Salih Is a 'Historic' Day: We Took Down the Conspiracy in 3 Days [Al-Houthi: Ightial Salih Yawm Tarikhi . . . Asqatna Al-Mu'amara fi 3 Ayam]," *Annahar*, December 4, 2017.

[13] Lucas Winter, "The Adaptive Transformation of Yemen's Republican Guard," *Small Wars Journal*, March 2017.

[14] Winter, 2017.

[15] Mark Mazzetti and David D. Kirkpatrick, "Saudi Arabia Leads Air Assault in Yemen," *New York Times*, March 25, 2015.

[16] Robert Beckhusen, "The Yemeni Air Force Probably No Longer Exists," *War Is Boring*, March 27, 2015.

[17] Michael Knights, "The Houthi War Machine: From Guerrilla War to State Capture," *CTC Sentinel*, September 2018.

[18] "The Houthis: The Military Reality and Sources of Support [Al-Huthiyun: Al-Haqiqa Al-'Askriya wa Masadir Al-Da'm]," Strategic Fiker Center for Studies, May 18, 2015. The 60 to 70 percent figure is also cited in Renad Mansour and Peter Salisbury, "Between Order and Chaos: A New Approach to Stalled State Transformations in Iraq and Yemen," *Chatham House*, September 2019.

movement are generally described as 'Houthis,' in reality the military structures in the country's northwest are a hybrid of the group's militias and the remnants of forces under the command of the pre-war interior and defence ministries along with other state institutions."[19]

Iran is the second source of the Houthis' statelike capabilities. At the time of the Houthis' takeover of Sanaa in 2015, Ambassador Gerald Feierstein assessed: "To the best of our understanding, the Houthis are not controlled directly by Iran. However, we have seen in recent years significant growth and expansion of Iranian engagement with the Houthis. We believe that Iran sees opportunities with the Houthis to expand its influence in Yemen and threaten Saudi and Gulf Arab interests. Iran provides financial support, weapons, training, and intelligence to the Houthis."[20] The full depth of Tehran's support to the Houthis is not public information. However, there is credible open-source reporting that Iran has provided the Houthis with small arms, landmines that the Houthis use both to fortify defensive positions and as improvised explosive devices (IEDs) to target government vehicles,[21] sea mines to prevent counterattacks on Houthi-controlled port infrastructure,[22] additional ballistic missile capability beyond those acquired from Yemen's military,[23] ballistic missile parts,[24] UAVs for ISR and lethal attack,[25] and remote-controlled watercraft used like UAVs for unmanned attack at sea.[26]

---

[19] Mansour and Salisbury, 2019.

[20] Gerald Feierstein, "Congressional Testimony Before the House Foreign Affairs Subcommittee on the Middle East and North Africa," April 14, 2015.

[21] "Dispatch from the Field: Mines and IEDs Employed by Houthi Forces on Yemen's West Coast," *Conflict Armament Research*, September 2018.

[22] "Dispatch from the Field: Mines and IEDs Employed by Houthi Forces on Yemen's West Coast," 2018.

[23] Asa Fitch, "How Yemen's Houthis Are Ramping Up Their Weapons Capability; Saudi Forces Have Intercepted More Than 100 Missiles Since 2015," *Wall Street Journal*, April 25, 2018.

[24] Fitch, 2018.

[25] Dhia Muhsin, "Houthi Use of Drones Delivers Potent Message in Yemen War," *IISS Blog*, August 27, 2019.

[26] "New Houthi Weapon Emerges: A Drone Boat," *Defense News*, February 19, 2017.

In addition, the Houthis appear to have adopted TTPs associated with Iran. This includes the aforementioned use of landmines as a component of IEDs, the use of UAVs equipped with bombs that explode by remote detonation or by preprogramming geographic coordinates,[27] and the Houthis' employment of coastal defense forces to target both merchant and military vessels in the Red Sea. Describing Iranian influence on Houthi TTPs for its maritime operations, Michael Knights observed,

> The Houthis took control of Yemen's coastal missile batteries and then integrated them into an Iranian-supported salvage and modernization program. Since 2015, Ansar Allah has attacked shipping with naval mines and anti-ship missiles that were already in the Yemeni arsenal, to which it has added the use of boat-mounted ATGMs. The Houthis developed around 30 coast-watcher stations, "spy dhows," drones, and the maritime radar of docked ships to create targeting solutions for attacks.[28]

Tactical and Operational Military Challenges

The military challenges posed by the Houthis are best divided into those that apply to the Saudi-led Coalition supporting the internationally recognized government in Yemen on the one hand and threats to the Gulf Cooperation Council (GCC) and, limitedly, the United States on the other. Because the Saudi-led Coalition operates within Yemeni territory, it is exposed to a broader range of threats than the United States, which has closed its embassy in Sanaa and only deploys forces and military systems inside Yemen in the form of occasional raids and drone strikes on al Qaeda in the Arabian Peninsula. The United States previously had a larger role in supporting the Saudi-led campaign in Yemen, although still from outside Yemen, that included broad targeting support and aerial refueling. Washington currently only provides targeting support for a small subset of threats that pertain to Saudi

---

[27] "Suicide Drones: Houthi Strategic Weapon," Abaad Studies and Research Center, January 2019.

[28] Knights, 2018.

and Emirati territory as well as maritime security. As of 2018, roughly 50 U.S. military personnel were involved in supporting Saudi efforts to suppress at least one of these threats—that posed by Houthi-controlled Theatre Ballistic Missiles.[29] The United States has ceased providing aerial refueling to the Saudi-led Coalition aircraft involved in strikes on Yemen.[30]

Tactical and Operational Military Challenges that Pertain to Yemeni Forces

Like many other proxy groups with statelike military capabilities, the Houthis primarily rely on a familiar array of conventional capabilities to target opposing military forces and civilian populations. Assessing the Houthis' siege of Taiz, a former Yemeni capital city often described as the state's industrial center, the United Nations Panel of Experts noted, "[Houthi] ground attacks involved the use of indirect-fire weapons such as mortars, artillery and rockets, as well as the use of tanks and anti-aircraft guns to hit ground targets."[31]

The Houthis and aligned forces have done great damage with indirect fire. In one of the deadlier attacks launched by Houthis against the Saudi-led Coalition operating in Yemen, a Houthi missile strike on a base in Marib killed 45 UAE soldiers and another five Bahraini soldiers.[32] In that strike, the Houthis used a Soviet-produced Tochka missile (NATO SS-21 Scarab).[33] By striking an ammunition site in which Coalition forces were not follow-

---

[29] Robert Karam, "Testimony to Senate Foreign Relations Committee from Former Assistant Secretary of Defense for International Security Affairs: U.S. Policy Towards Yemen," video, C-Span, April 17, 2018 (minute 1:17); Helene Cooper, Thomas Gibbons-Neff, and Eric Schmitt, "Army Special Forces Secretly Help Saudis Combat Threat from Yemen Rebels," *New York Times*, May 3, 2018.

[30] Phil Stewart, "U.S. Halting Refueling of Saudi-Led Coalition Aircraft in Yemen's War," Reuters, November 9, 2018.

[31] Human Rights Council, "Situation of Human Rights in Yemen, Including Violations and Abuses Since September 2014," website, September 2019.

[32] Kareem Fahim, "Houthi Rebels Kill 45 U.A.E. Soldiers in Yemen Fighting," *New York Times*, September 4, 2015.

[33] Sébastien Roblin, "SS-21 Scarab: Russia's Forgotten (But Deadly) Ballistic Missile," *National Interest*, September 12, 2016b.

ing best practices of sufficiently separating their forces from ammunition stores, the Houthis maximized casualties. Later in 2015, UAE-operated Patriot batteries based in Marib were able to intercept three Houthi missiles attempting to execute a similar attack.[34]

In addition to indirect-fire weapons, Houthi-aligned forces also employ direct fire in the form of tank attacks. The authors do not have data that break out the percentage of Houthi attacks of this type, but the Houthis' use of armor appears to have declined over the course of the civil war. Many of the Houthis' notable uses of armor occurred in 2015 during its initial push through central and southern governorates.[35] Since then, there has been less reporting on Houthis' use of armor in the conflict. That may be because tanks were vulnerable to the Saudi-led Coalition air attacks and thus have been destroyed or rendered inoperable by strikes.[36] It could also be that the Houthis are using tanks to defend and reinforce territory rather than launch offensives and have successfully concealed them.[37] In January 2020, around 40 Houthi tanks were reported destroyed by the Coalition.[38] It is not clear how many tanks Houthi forces possess, but it appears that the group continues to hold them in its arsenal.

---

[34] Missile Defense Project, "Interactive: The Missile War in Yemen," Missile Threat, *Center for Strategic and International Studies*, December 10, 2019.

[35] Mohammed Mukhashaf, "Yemen Houthi Fighters Backed by Tanks Reach Central Aden," Reuters, April 1, 2015; Knights, 2018; Ali al-Mujahed and Hugh Laylor, "Saudi-Led Airstrikes Intensify in Yemen as Possible Coalition Land Attack Looms," *Washington Post*, March 28, 2015.

[36] For more on the destruction of Houthi tanks, see "Saudi-Led Strikes Drive Houthis from Aden," *Al Jazeera*, April 3, 2015; "Saudi-Led Airstrikes Kill 15 at Wedding in Yemen, Witnesses Say," *Wall Street Journal*, October 7, 2015.

[37] For evidence of continued use and possession of tanks by Houthis after 2015, see Noah Browning and Sami Aboudi, "Former President Saleh Dead after Switching Sides in Yemen's Civil War," Reuters, December 4, 2017; Ahmed Al-Haj, "Fighting Sharply Rises in Yemen, Endangering Peace Efforts," Associated Press, January 29, 2020; Nadwa Al-Dawsari, "Running Around in Circles: How Saudi Arabia Is Losing Its War in Yemen to Iran," Middle East Institute, March 3, 2020; and "A Long Fight Ahead: The Army Is Gaining the Upper Hand in Yemen's Civil War: Still, No End Is Near," *The Economist*, January 4, 2018.

[38] Al-Haj, 2020.

In addition to these relatively common land-force capabilities, the Houthis have also displayed the ability to employ UASs for reconnaissance and attack. The Houthis are believed to have acquired some UAS systems through commercial purchase, and others are suspected to have been provided by Iran.[39] In its review of Houthi UAVs and UAV components, Conflict Armament Research concluded, "Many components either originated in Iran or are used by Iranian-backed groups in the region," though it does appear that the Houthis began domestic production of components for one of its UAVs by 2018.[40]

The first UAV known to be within the Houthi arsenal was a DJI Phantom that was first documented in use by Houthi forces in December 2015. It appears that for the first two years of the Yemeni Civil War, the Houthis predominantly relied on commercial-grade drones to conduct ISR operations in Yemen.[41] The Houthis have expanded their ISR UAV arsenal to include the Hudhud, Hudhud-1, Raqib, and Rased UAV models.[42] UAVs are used by the Houthis to locate opposition forces prior to launching ground attacks and to "[c]orrect artillery course."[43]

Evidence suggests that Iran has transferred Iranian-produced Qasef-1 UAVs[44] and components of both Shahed 123 UAVs[45] and Qasef-1 UAVs[46]

---

[39] "Armed Drones Are a Growing Threat from Rebels in Yemen," *Wall Street Journal Video,* May 2, 2019.

[40] "Dispatch from the Field," 2020.

[41] Muhsin, 2019; Ahmed Himmiche, Fernando Rosenfeld Carvajal, Dakshinie Ruwanthika Gunaratne, Gregory Johnsen, and Adrian Wilkinson, "Letter Dated 26 January 2018 from the Panel of Experts on Yemen Mandated by Security Council Resolution 2342 (2017) Addressed to the President of the Security Council," United Nations Security Council, January 26, 2018.

[42] "Evolution of UAVs Employed by Houthi Forces in Yemen," *Conflict Armament Research*, February 2020.

[43] "Suicide Drones," 2019.

[44] "'Kamikaze' Drones Used by Houthi Forces to Attack Coalition Missile Defence Systems," *Conflict Armament Research*, March 2017.

[45] Brian Hook, "Iran Regime's Transfer of Arms to Proxy Groups & On," U.S. Department of State, YouTube, November 29, 2018.

[46] Himmiche et al., 2018.

to the Houthis since 2015. The Qasef-1, while claimed to be fully manu-factured domestically by the Houthis, is strongly believed to be of Iranian origin as it is "virtually identical in design, dimensions and capability to that of the Ababil-T, manufactured by the Iranian Aircraft Manufactur-ing Industries."[47] It appears that the Houthis have assembled some of their Qasef-1 UAV arsenal inside Yemen, but a United Nations team concluded that many of the components required for the assembly of the Qasef-1 have "emanated from the Islamic Republic of Iran."[48]

Between the time the Houthis were first observed launching armed drones in 2018 through January 2020, the Houthis executed more than 100 UAS attacks.[49] Among the more notable attacks, the Houthis are believed to be the first nonstate actor to use a drone to assassinate a state official, which they accomplished in January 2019 when they killed the Yemeni gov-ernment's deputy Army chief of staff in a UAV attack alongside five other members of the Yemeni Army at al-Anad base.[50] Particularly concerning, the Houthis have shown an ability to launch coordinated missile and drone strikes, twice executing large-casualty events with this approach. Those events included its August 2019 attack on a military parade in Aden that killed more than 30 and its January 2020 attack on a military training site in Marib that killed more than 100.[51]

Tactical and Operational Military Challenges That Pertain to Saudi-Led Coalition and U.S. Forces
Ballistic and Cruise Missile Capabilities
The Houthis possess an array of ballistic missiles that they have employed against government and Saudi-led Coalition forces inside Yemen (as noted

---

[47] Himmiche et al., 2018.

[48] Himmiche et al., 2018.

[49] Caleb Weiss, "Houthis Kill Over 100 Yemeni Soldiers in Missile, Drone Attack on Base," *Long War Journal*, January 20, 2020.

[50] "Armed Drones Are a Growing Threat from Rebels in Yemen," 2019; Nick Waters, "Houthis Use Armed Drone to Target Yemeni Army Top Brass," *Bellingcat*, January 10, 2019.

[51] Weiss, 2020.

in the section above), as well as against Saudi, Emirati, and, in October 2016, U.S. targets outside Yemen. Data from CSIS' Missile Defense Project, which tracks missile strikes against Saudi Arabia from the start of the Coalition's intervention in Yemen (March 2015) through the end of 2019, revealed 134 separate attacks against Saudi ground targets, some including multiple missile salvos.[52] Both Saudi civilian and military air base infrastructure are a frequent target of attacks, including King Khalid air base at Khamis Mushayt. These missile attacks are delivered by Scuds that were part of the Yemeni military's arsenal, as well as Iranian-provided missiles that have a longer flight range, up to 600 miles, allowing the Houthis to target Riyadh and other locations deep in Saudi Arabia.[53] It is believed these missiles were delivered by Iran to the Houthis in pieces and then reassembled inside Yemen.[54] Examples of projectiles that Iran is believed to have provided include Qiam-1 short-range ballistic missiles,[55] Sayyad 2C surface-to-air missiles, Toophan antitank missiles,[56] and Borkan-2H short-range ballistic missiles.[57] Figure 6.1 provides a rough indication of the effectiveness of Houthi missile attacks against ground targets outside of Yemen, based on data from the CSIS Missile Defense Project. According to that data, the large majority of attacks were intercepted by U.S.-manufactured missile defense systems. Without access to such sophisticated technologies, it appears that the toll of the Houthi strikes would have been much higher.

In addition to this ballistic missile capability, the Houthis have also employed cruise missiles against maritime targets, albeit much less frequently than their ballistic missile attacks on ground targets in Saudi Arabia. The CSIS data flags three attacks on UAE vessels, two on Saudi ves-

---

[52] Missile Defense Project, 2019.

[53] Knights, 2018.

[54] Knights, 2018.

[55] Daniel Brown, "The Pentagon Showed Off These Weapons That Iran Has Given to the Taliban and Houthis, Saying It Wasn't a Political Stunt," *Business Insider*, November 30, 2018.

[56] Hook, 2018.

[57] Himmiche et al., 2018.

FIGURE 6.1

Houthi Missile Attacks Against Ground Targets Outside of Yemen

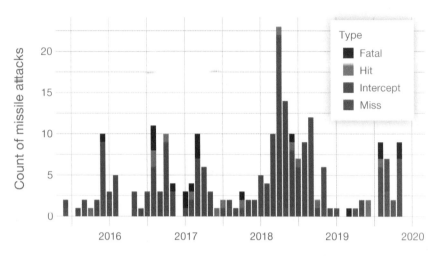

SOURCE: CSIS Missile Defense Project.

sels, and one on a U.S. naval ship; several of these attacks involved suspected Houthi use of cruise missile capabilities.[58]

The Houthis' anti-ship missiles appear to have initially been primarily made up of stockpiles the Yemeni military possessed prior to the outbreak of the war in 2015. In 2017, a United Nations panel of experts expected that this stockpile would eventually be depleted "as long as the arms embargo is effective in ensuring that there is no resupply of anti-ship missiles."[59] It appears that since then, the number of attacks continued, but by the end of 2018 had mostly dissipated,[60] perhaps indicating that the Houthis had used up their stockpile and had neither developed a replacement of their own nor

---

[58] Missile Defense Project, 2019.

[59] Ahmed Himmiche, Dakshinie Ruwanthika Gunaratne, Gregory Johnsen, and Adrian Wilkinson, "Letter Dated 27 January 2017 from the Panel of Experts on Yemen Addressed to the President of the Security Council," United Nations Security Council, January 31, 2017.

[60] Caleb Weiss, "Analysis: Houthi Naval Attacks in the Red Sea," *Long War Journal*, August 17, 2019b.

gained access to regular new stock from an external supplier. It does appear that for a time Iran provided the Houthis with its Noor anti-ship missiles. Evidence from an attack on a Saudi ship in 2018 suggested the Houthis may have used a Noor missile in the attack.[61] It is possible that the Houthis are receiving these missiles with the intent of using them against targets at sea, are repurposing these projectiles for other elements of its campaign, or have found another means of attacking maritime targets preferable to using missiles.

The Houthis have utilized their missile capabilities in direct confrontations with the United States. In October 2016, Houthi forces engaged in three separate missile attacks on the United States Ship (USS) *Mason* off the coast of Yemen. On October 3, 2016, the USS *Mason* and two other U.S. warships, USS *Nitze* and USS *Ponce*, began operating off the coast of Yemen after a Houthi attack on October 1, 2016, against the *Swift*, a UAE vessel, in the Bab al-Mandab Strait.[62] On October 9, 2016, Houthi forces fired two missiles at the *Mason*. To counter the projectiles, the *Mason* deployed two Standard Missile 2 interceptors, a RIM-162 Evolved Sea Sparrow Missile, and a Nulka decoy. It is unclear whether these countermeasures prevented the *Mason* from being hit or if the Houthis missed, but neither missile hit the *Mason*.[63] On October 12, 2016, Houthi forces fired a missile at the *Mason* in the Bab al-Mandab Strait. The *Mason* intercepted and destroyed this projectile using countermeasures.[64] Hours later, the USS *Nitze* responded to the

---

[61] Ahmed Himmiche, Fernando Rosenfeld Carvajal, Wolf-Christian Paes, Henry Thompson, and Marie-Louise Tougas, "Letter Dated 25 January 2019 from the Panel of Experts on Yemen Addressed to the President of the Security Council," United Nations Security Council, "January 29, 2019.

[62] Alex Almeida, Jeremy Vaughan, and Michael Knights, "Houthi Antishipping Attacks in the Bab al-Mandab Strait," The Washington Institute, October 6, 2016; Jeremy Vaughan, Michael Eisenstadt, and Michael Knights, "Missile Attacks on the USS Mason: Principles to Guide U.S. Response," The Washington Institute, October 12, 2016; "Yemen: Houthis Claim Attack on UAE Military Vessel," *Al Jazeera*, October 2, 2016.

[63] Vaughan, Eisenstadt, and Knights, 2016; Phil Stewart, "U.S. Navy Ship Targeted in Failed Missile Attack from Yemen: U.S.," Reuters, October 9, 2016.

[64] Tara Copp, "Aegis Defense System Helped Stop Missile Attack on USS Mason," *Stars and Stripes*, October 13, 2016.

missile attacks on the USS *Mason* by launching Tomahawk cruise missiles at three Houthi radar sites. All three radar sites were destroyed.[65] On October 15, 2016, Houthi forces fired an unknown number of missiles at the USS *Mason*. The *Mason* detected the Houthi strikes and was not struck by the projectiles, though the countermeasures employed by the USS *Mason* are not publicly known.[66] These attempted Houthi strikes on the USS *Mason*, while failures, indicate that Houthi missile capabilities have been and could continue to be a direct threat to U.S. and allied naval forces.

UAS Capabilities

The Houthis possess both commercial- and military-grade UAVs. By September 2016, the Houthis were in possession of Qasef-1 UAVs,[67] which are a type of combat UAV. Since 2016, their arsenal of combat UAVs has included the Qasef-2K, Sammad-2, and Sammad-3 UAVs.[68] Houthi forces have weaponized some of their UAVs by crashing into targets[69] or by detonating them[70] to "rain shrapnel down on [their] target[s]."[71] Houthi forces have utilized the Qasef-1 to target Coalition Patriot missile systems,[72] and, in January 2019, they targeted senior figures of the Yemeni Army at al-Anad base,[73] where

---

[65] Phil Stewart, "U.S. Military Strikes Yemen after Missile Attacks on U.S. Navy Ship," Reuters, October 12, 2016; "Yemen Conflict: US Strikes Radar Sites after Missile Attack on ship," BBC News, October 13, 2016.

[66] "Yemen War: US Ship Faces New Round of 'Houthi Missiles,'" *Al Jazeera*, October 16, 2016; Missile Defense Project, 2019.

[67] Himmiche et al., 2018.

[68] "Evolution of UAVs Employed by Houthi Forces in Yemen," 2020.

[69] "Iranian Technology Transfers to Yemen," *Conflict Armament Research*, March 2017; Himmiche et al., 2018.

[70] Waters, 2019.

[71] "Houthi Rebel Drone Kills Several at Saudi Coalition Parade," *France 24*, October 1, 2019.

[72] "Iranian Technology Transfers to Yemen," 2017.

[73] Waters, 2019.

the Houthis claimed their targets had been "personnel from the Saudi-led coalition backing the government."[74]

Additionally, the Houthis have utilized their UAV arsenal in attacks against their adversaries outside of Yemen in Saudi Arabia and, quite possibly, the UAE. In April 2018, Houthi forces began using its UAVs to attack targets in southwestern Saudi Arabia in the provinces of Jizan, Asir, and Najran. It appears that these attacks increased in frequency in 2019 and have continued into 2020. Houthi drones have targeted airports, infrastructure, and troops inside Saudi Arabia. The actual occurrence of and the scope of damage from these attacks is unclear.[75]

There is no clear or complete public dataset of the total number or location of Houthi UAV attacks outside of Yemen. The Houthis often falsely claim to have carried out attacks, and local governments often do not acknowledge the occurrence of attacks. The information environment renders the exact number of Houthi UAV attacks against the UAE and Saudi Arabia outside of Yemen unclear, but the threat to GCC interests in their home countries is real.

Fitting into the Houthis' tendency to release what appear to be false attack claims, the group has at times taken credit for attacks that appear to have been carried out by others. In an interesting twist and indication of increased Iranian influence, the Houthis used their demonstrated capability of coordinated missile and drone strikes to falsely claim that they executed the attack on Saudi Aramco at Abqaiq and Khurais in September 2019.[76] The United States has rejected that claim, suggesting that Iran executed the strike from Iranian territory[77] or that an Iranian proxy in Iraq carried out the attack. The origin of this attack remains unclear, but it appears that the

---

[74] "Yemen Soldiers Killed in Houthi Drone Attack on Base," BBC News, January 10, 2019.

[75] Weiss, 2019a.

[76] "Houthi Drone Attacks on 2 Saudi Aramco Oil Facilities Spark Fires," *Al Jazeera*, September 14, 2019.

[77] Humeyra Pamuk, "Exclusive: U.S. Probe of Saudi oil Attack Shows It Came from North—Report," Reuters, December 19, 2019.

attacks did not originate from Yemen.[78] Although the Houthis might have used the strike to rally their supporters and recruit among those who blame Saudi airstrikes for the country's insecurity, it is hard to imagine that these benefits would have outweighed the additional risk incurred by that claim if it had been accepted. This suggests that the Houthis' reliance on Iranian support is such that they are willing to accept additional military pressure in return for Tehran's assistance.

Air Defense Capabilities

The Houthis have had access to air defense systems and units since January 2015, when many Saleh loyalists belonging to air-defense brigades in Sana'a joined Houthi forces. In the months that followed, the Houthi-Saleh coalition gained some support from other air-defense brigades in the country, but more significant was the acquisition of much of the air-defense equipment that had belonged to the Yemeni Air Force that allowed the formation of seven Houthi-Saleh air-defense brigades by late March 2015.[79]

In March 2015, the Coalition initiated its campaign against Houthi-Saleh forces on behalf of the Hadi government and initiated a "major suppression-of-enemy-air-defenses campaign,"[80] eliminating a significant amount of Houthi-Saleh air-defense systems by mid-April 2015. Houthi-Saleh forces attempted to counter this campaign with surface-to-air missiles but appear to have largely failed to inflict significant, if any, damage to Coalition air forces. Houthi-Saleh forces were more effective in utilizing shoulder-launched air-defense weapons to destroy Coalition aircraft and UAVs. As the war progressed, Houthi-Saleh forces created their Missile Research and Development Center (MRDC), which converted existing Houthi-Saleh surface-to-air missiles "from the S-75/SA-2 system into ballistic missiles."[81] By 2016, it seems that Houthi-Saleh forces lacked significant air-defense sys-

---

[78] Dion Nissenbaum, Summer Said, and Nancy A. Youssef, "Suspicions Rise That Saudi Oil Attack Came from Outside Yemen," *Wall Street Journal*, September 14, 2019.

[79] Tom Cooper, "The Houthis' Do-It-Yourself Air Defenses: Part Two," *War Is Boring*, January 16, 2018a; Farzin Nadimi and Michael Knights, "Iran's Support to Houthi Air Defenses in Yemen," The Washington Institute, April 4, 2018.

[80] Cooper, 2018a.

[81] Cooper, 2018a.

tems and were being regularly targeted by the Coalition with air strikes[82] and thus were in need of developing or acquiring better resources beyond the portable air-defense systems that Houthi-Saleh forces retained.[83]

MRDC developed a means to convert air-to-air infrared homing missiles into SAMs. Launching systems were then developed and mounted onto the back of pickup trucks. By February 2017, these systems had been deployed into the field. It is unclear how successful these weapons have been in targeting Coalition aircraft. To improve accuracy of these weapons, MRDC "found a solution by coupling one of three U.S.-made Flir Systems ULTRA 8500 turrets, delivered to Yemen back in 2008, with makeshift controls for their 'new' SAMs."[84] Houthi-Saleh forces deployed this coupled system by November 2017. On January 7, 2018, one of these SAMs nearly struck a Saudi F-15.[85]

Beyond the inherited, seized, and retrofitted air-defense systems that the Houthis had, it appears that Iran supplied the group with such missiles as the Iranian Sayyad 2C surface-to-air missiles,[86] which can be utilized for air defense.[87] Iran has also provided the group with virtual radar receivers that could allow Houthi forces to "launch dangerous 'pop-up' attacks in which operators use passive systems to track a target and then launch a missile in the right direction; the missile's infrared or radar guidance system does not activate until it nears the target."[88] These radar receivers could also

---

[82] Cooper, 2018a.

[83] Tom Cooper, "The Houthis' Do-It-Yourself Air Defenses: Part Three," *War Is Boring*, January 23, 2018b.

[84] Cooper, 2018b.

[85] Cooper, 2018b; Nadimi and Knights, 2018.

[86] Himmiche et al., 2018; Hook, 2018.

[87] Farzin Nadimi, "Iran Develops Air Defense Capability for Possible Regional Role," The Washington Institute, August 27, 2019; Behnam Ben Taleblu, "Analysis: An Iranian SAM in the Arabian Peninsula," *Long War Journal*, April 2, 2018; Jeremy Binnie, "Iran Rolls Out Another Medium-Range SAM," *Jane's*, November 12, 2013.

[88] Nadimi and Knights, 2018.

improve the capabilities of the air-to-air missiles that the MRDC converts into SAMs.[89]

There are similar issues with creating an accurate picture of the amount of damage inflicted on Coalition forces by Houthi air-defense systems as there are calculating that from Houthi UAVs. Despite the uncertainty around the amount of damage that the Houthis inflicted on the Saudi-led Coalition's air forces using their air-defense systems, it has been confirmed that the group shot down a number of American UAVs. Houthi forces shot down American MQ-9 Reaper drones on October 1, 2017;[90] June 6, 2019;[91] and August 20, 2019.[92] Houthi success targeting American UAVs indicates that the group is a risk to American equipment and could potentially affect the ability of the U.S. to conduct UAV strikes and surveillance in Yemen.

Maritime Capabilities

Since 2015, Houthi forces have engaged in targeting commercial shipping and warships in the Red Sea. Outside of the use of anti-ship missiles noted earlier, the Houthis have used sea mines and water-borne improvised explosive devices (WBIEDs) against targets at sea. Evidence suggests that some of the Houthis' maritime capabilities come from the Yemeni government's stockpile from before the start of the war,[93] as well as elements that they have developed themselves,[94] and they have also been given assistance and supplies by Iran.[95]

---

[89] Cooper, 2018b; Nadimi and Knights, 2018.

[90] Shawn Snow, "US MQ-9 Drone Shot Down in Yemen," *Defense News*, October 2, 2017.

[91] "CENTCOM: MQ-9 Reaper Shot Down Over Yemen Last Week," *Military Times*, June 16, 2019.

[92] Joshua Karsten, "Houthi Rebels in Yemen Claim to Shoot Down US Drone," *Stars and Stripes*, August 21, 2019.

[93] Himmiche et al., 2017.

[94] "Mines and IEDs Employed by Houthi Forces on Yemen's West Coast," *Conflict Armament Research*, September 2018.

[95] Weiss, 2019b.

By January 2017, the Houthis had begun using WBIEDs to target vessels in the Red Sea.[96] Since then, the Houthis have regularly used these WBIEDs to target commercial ships and warships.[97] Some of these WBIEDs appear to have been made by modifying patrol boats that the UAE donated to the Yemeni Navy prior to the current conflict. A Conflict Armament Research report from 2017 did not find evidence suggesting "direct Iranian involvement in the device's construction, but suggests that certain components were sourced from Iran or through Iranian channels."[98] Since 2017, the Houthis have developed WBIEDs resembling fishing boats that "could be more easily hidden, and harder to identify as a threat. It may also make it cheaper to build since existing fishing vessels can be converted."[99] The rising use of these vessels and the development of WBIEDs looking more like civilian fishing vessels could make it more difficult for targets to distinguish between civilian watercraft and WBIEDs that may, in turn, lead to a decline in averted attacks or inadvertent targeting of civilians by conventional forces.

The Houthis have deployed a mixture of conventional and improvised sea mines[100] off Yemen's Red Sea coast since 2016.[101] Conflict Armament Research could not determine the exact origin of the naval mines utilized by the Houthis but noted that a United Nations panel of experts believed them to be of Soviet origin.[102] It is also believed that some of these naval mines were produced by Iran.[103] The Houthis use naval mines "despite the risk to

[96] "New Houthi Weapon Emerges," 2017; "Anatomy of a 'Drone Boat,'" *Conflict Armament Research*, December 2017.

[97] Weiss, 2019b.

[98] "Anatomy of a 'Drone Boat,'" 2017.

[99] H. I. Sutton, "Disguised Explosive Boat May Be New Threat to Tankers off Yemen," *Forbes*, March 4, 2020.

[100] "Mines and IEDs Employed by Houthi Forces on Yemen's West Coast," 2018.

[101] "Special Advisory: Naval Mines and MBIEDs off Yemen," *NYA International*, May 19, 2017.

[102] "Mines and IEDs Employed by Houthi Forces on Yemen's West Coast," 2018.

[103] "Special Advisory," 2017.

commercial, fishing, and aid vessels."[104] These mines have inflicted damage on civilian watercraft and military vessels and have caused both civilian and military casualties.[105] It is unclear whether these mines have caused significant damage to the Coalition's navies, but the Coalition has worked to clear mines from the Red Sea's waters.[106]

The risk of future confrontations involving Houthi maritime capabilities is likely heightened by the recent use of mining, suspected by Islamic Revolutionary Guard Corps naval forces, of merchant ships in the Persian Gulf and Gulf of Oman. Should the Houthis follow the lead of their state sponsor, the Red Sea is a potential site for horizontal escalation that would stretch U.S. resources.

Coalition Responses: Standoff Fires and Proxies

The relatively high level of capabilities possessed by Houthi forces has shaped the way that the Saudi-led Coalition has intervened in the conflict. Rather than risk high casualties on the ground, the Coalition has preferred to use standoff fires, primarily from the air, or to work through its own proxy ground forces. The results can be seen in indiscriminate fires in which Coalition air forces have been challenged to identify and prosecute Houthi military targets while avoiding civilian harm. The United Nations Panel of Experts concluded in a 2020 investigation of several problematic strikes that "in all cases investigated, the information and evidence gathered by the Panel lead to the conclusion that it is likely that the principles of distinction, precaution or proportionality were not respected."[107]

---

[104] "Yemen: Houthi Landmines Kill Civilians, Block Aid," *Human Rights Watch*, April 22, 2019.

[105] "Special Advisory," 2017; "Houthi Naval Mine Reportedly Kills Three Egyptian Fshermen in Red Sea," *Almasdar Online*, March 24, 2020; "Naval Mine Kills Yemeni Coastguards in Bab al-Mandeb," *Al Arabiya English*, March 11, 2017.

[106] "Watch: Yemeni Army Detonates Six Mines Planted by Houthis in Red Sea," *Al Arabiya English*, August 25, 2018; "Saudi Naval Forces Clear Houthi Mines from Hodeida Coast," *Al Arabiya English*, March 26, 2017.

[107] United Nations Panel of Experts on Yemen, "Letter to the President of the Security Council," S/2020/70, January 27, 2020.

Not surprisingly, these tactics have alienated local populations. In an August 2019 survey conducted by the Yemen Polling Center, "airstrikes" were selected as the second-greatest threat to respondents' personal security, polling well ahead of "Houthi fighter threats." And in the north of the country, where Saudi strikes are most concentrated, "airstrikes" were judged by respondents as the greatest threat to their personal security overall, eclipsing even general categories such as "war continuity" and "poverty and disease." [108] According to one recent report, the end result is self-defeating for the Saudis: "[C]ivilian casualties as a result of airstrikes create resentment against the government and the coalition, playing into the hands of the Houthis. . . . 'Instead of helping the tribes, the coalition is pushing them toward the Houthis with these airstrikes,' said a local tribesman."[109] It also appears that these standoff strikes are reducing support for the Saudis' local partners, with the Republic of Yemen Government generally, and President Hadi particularly, losing popular support from their association with them.[110]

Strategic Military Challenges

After five years of war, the Houthis' position in Yemen is arguably stronger than that of the internationally recognized government. Specifically, the Houthis control the capital city; have launched an offensive against the strategic Marib governorate; and are continuing to lay siege to Taiz, a large city in the south of the country. It does not appear that the Houthi threat will dissipate in the near term, and it could very well escalate to force war termination on more favorable terms to the movement. Despite the United Nations weapons embargo and routine interceptions of weapons and component shipments to the Houthis, the organization appears to continue

---

[108] Yemen Polling Center, "Perceptions of the Yemeni Public on Security-Related Issues: Survey Findings, Sanaa/Aden," August 2019.

[109] Al-Dawsari, 2020.

[110] Christopher J. Le Mon, "Moving from Partisan to Peacemaker in Yemen," in Andrew Miller and Dafna Rand, eds., *Reengaging the Middle East*, Washington, D.C.: Brookings, 2020, p. 52.

receiving shipments from Iran based on its use of these weapons and components in its war effort.

Meanwhile, the internationally recognized government is highly fractured, has effectively ceded control of Aden to southern separatists, lost the commitment of one of its most important backers (the UAE), and could see Saudi Arabia change its calculus after years of stalemate and international criticism. While once determined to seize Al-Hodeidah, a port that provides the Houthis an economic lifeline, and the high ground above Sanaa from which it could threaten Houthi control of the capital with indirect fire, today Saudi-backed forces are far from achieving those objectives. It is also unclear whether Saudi Arabia will continue to judge the costs of the operation as worthwhile in light of the significant drop in international oil prices.

Externally, the United States has limited its involvement in the conflict to defending the security of its GCC partners. Because the mission is highly circumscribed in scope, those activities appear sustainable. However, they do come at the cost of allocating some high-demand/low-density assets, such as point missile defense and Carrier assets, to a peripheral threat relative to the United States' global national security interests. The mission is also highly unpopular in Congress, which has acted to limit U.S. involvement in Yemen in light of criticism over Saudi conduct of the air campaign and general disapproval with human rights under the Kingdom since Mohammad Bin Salman's accession as Crown Prince.[111]

Conclusion: The Houthis' Ability to Outlast Foreign Interveners

Since the start of the Yemeni Civil War in 2015, the Houthis have demonstrated the capacity to wage war against the militaries of the internationally recognized government of Yemen and its state allies. Initially much of the Houthis' capabilities were accumulated through their alliance with Saleh-loyalists in the Yemeni military and through pilfering existing Yemeni

---

[111] Including, notably, the murder of *Washington Post* columnist Jamal Khashoggi at a Saudi consulate in Istanbul in October 2018 (Ben Hubbard, "Saudi Death Sentences in Khashoggi Killing Fail to Dispel Questions," *New York Times*, December 23, 2019).

weapons stocks, but as the war continued, the Houthis developed a weapons manufacturing capability and a supply line of materiel, components, and advanced systems from Iran. The Houthis have proven themselves a threat to U.S. allies, international commerce, civilian life, and, to a limited extent, U.S. forces and assets through both their direct and indirect attacks on military, civilian, commercial targets. Although the Houthis do not appear to have been as dependent on Iranian support for their military capabilities as the VNSAs in the other case studies in this report, Iran does appear to have provided the Houthis with financial and military support. In particular, Tehran appears to have provided the Houthis with landmines, sea mines, ballistic missiles, UAVs for ISR and lethal attack, and remote-controlled watercraft used in unmanned attacks at sea.

At the tactical and operational levels, the dynamics of combat in Yemen appear similar to many other cases of state-supported VNSAs. Despite being nonstate actors, the Houthis have access to a wide range of fairly sophisticated military capabilities. The complexity of the military challenge that they present is illustrated through such actions as their adaptation of existing missile systems and components to new purposes in the civil war. On the other side of the conflict, the Saudi-led Coalition has behaved very similarly to other states attempting to limit their casualties when intervening in an intrastate conflict against a relatively sophisticated adversary. It has relied overwhelmingly on standoff fires and other tactics that have alienated the local population, helping to reinforce popular support for the Houthis in the regions they control.

At the strategic level, the Yemen case illustrates the limitations of the United States' reliance on local partners. It may never have been realistic to expect the internationally recognized government to fare well militarily against the Houthis, especially once they aligned with elements of the former Saleh government. But even the more capable militaries of Saudi Arabia and the UAE have had very limited success against the Houthis.

The case also exhibits how the relative time horizons of the conflict actors present dilemmas for the military intervention. Because the Houthis are fighting on their own soil and Iran has not committed forces to the conflict, there are few time pressures that require this side of the conflict to achieve their objectives quickly or revisit their strategy. On the other hand, the internationally recognized government is reliant on a direct military intervention by outside states to sustain even its current level of success against the Houthis. This creates more time pressure for the government's external backers to achieve their war aims or reduce their intervention to save resources.

CHAPTER 7

Conclusion: Synthesis of Findings and Policy Recommendations

In this chapter, we summarize the findings of this report, focusing first on the military implications of proxy warfare for the United States military and then drawing lessons for potential future contingencies.[1] Notably, our findings are based on only four cases, obviously limiting the generalizability of our results. And, indeed, as discussed in the overview of our research approach in Chapter 2, these four cases were chosen to represent particularly capable insurgencies. They do, however, provide an indication of the *potential* capabilities of state-supported VNSAs (albeit likely at the high end of spectrum), which is perhaps more useful in many ways to defense planners than understanding what the average case looks like.

Tactical- and Operational-Level Challenges

The case-study chapters in this report provide evidence of the potential increased lethality of nonstate actors when they are supported by states. In the First Indochina War, for instance, the Chinese-supported Vietminh were able to defeat more than 10,000 French soldiers in a pitched battle at Dien Bien Phu using dozens of howitzers, Katyusha rocket launchers, antiaircraft artillery, and thousands of tons of ammunition. Although Dien Bien Phu was among the most spectacular successes of state-supported VNSAs, it is

---

[1]   Our implications for the future are not limited to a specific date range. In broad terms, we expect the lessons from our research to be applicable through at least 2035, the period currently being used for long-term defense planning.

not unique. The Russian-led separatist forces (RLSF) in Ukraine between 2014 and 2022 used heavy weaponry (including tanks and antitank guided missiles) to destroy an estimated two-thirds of the AFU's armored vehicles, and sophisticated RLSF air defense capabilities at one point had effectively neutralized Ukrainian air power. The Houthis have used Iranian-supplied ballistic missiles to impose costs on Saudi Arabia and the UAE by striking targets hundreds of miles away from Houthi positions. The electronic and cyber warfare practiced by RLSF provide some indication of the level of sophistication that VNSAs today can achieve when supported by a major power. As Table 7.1 illustrates, the air defenses, anti-armor weapons, artillery, mines, and other weaponry used so effectively by the VNSAs in our case studies are not unique to these cases; they have been employed by a great many other groups over the years.

Complexity of Ground Operations

Consistent with the first proposition we outlined in Chapter 2, the case studies in this report suggest that state-supported VNSAs pose a complex set of

TABLE 7.1

Examples of State-Supported VNSA Military Capabilities

VNSA Capability	Examples
SHORAD	• Houthis • *Contras* • *Afghan mujahideen* • RLSF • Vietminh
ATGMs/anti-armor weapons	• RLSF • *Lebanese Hezbollah* • *Hamas* • *Iraqi Shiite militias*
Artillery	• RLSF • Vietminh
Mining	• Vietcong • *Iraqi Shiite militias* • *ZANLA*

NOTE: Italicized examples do not appear in the case studies in this report but feature in the broader literature on state-supported VNSAs.

tactical- to operational-level challenges to the United States and other forces that oppose them. The French in Indochina, for instance, were never able to meet the twin challenges of massing to defeat the highly capable Vietminh and dispersing to prevent them from controlling the countryside and isolating French garrisons. Military experts still debate whether the United States should have focused on the more conventional threat posed by the NVA or the irregular threat posed by the Vietcong, but the United States clearly had trouble doing both, using weaponry and tactics for the one that were ill suited to the other.[2] Nor were these militaries alone in finding these challenges difficult. The Israeli Defense Forces (IDF) that were well adapted to the Second Intifada were initially poorly suited to the hybrid threat posed by Lebanese Hezbollah.[3] In short, state-supported VNSAs appear to pose a complex challenge for which neither militaries focused solely on high-intensity conventional warfare (such as the United States at the outset of the war in Vietnam) nor those focused on low-intensity irregular warfare (such as the IDF in Lebanon) are well prepared.

Targeting Dilemmas

Chapter 2 suggested that militaries fighting state-supported VNSAs may face difficult targeting dilemmas. One way for such militaries to try to offset the advanced capabilities of certain state-supported VNSAs is through extensive use of standoff fires, including air power and longer-range ground fires. But in doing so, these militaries risk alienating local public opinion through the increased risk of deaths among noncombatants.

The case studies in this report suggest that many capable militaries fighting counterinsurgencies did indeed come to rely heavily on standoff fires in an effort to reduce their own casualties—even at the cost of alienating local populations. The French, for instance, used "massive" amounts of napalm and other fires in their war against the Vietminh years before

---

[2]   Summers, 1995; Andrew F. Krepinevich, Jr., *The Army and Vietnam*, Baltimore, Md.: Johns Hopkins University Press, 1986.

[3]   Johnson, 2010; Johnson, 2011.

the United States employed similar tactics in the country.[4] Dartmouth University political scientist Benjamin Valentino has estimated that the French were responsible for between 60,000 and 250,000 deaths in their campaign against the Vietminh.[5] Similarly, the United States in its own war in Vietnam, the Saudis and Emiratis in Yemen, and the Ukrainian government in the Donbas War from 2014 to 2022 all employed fires in ways that were often described as indiscriminate and that turned much of local opinion against the counterinsurgents. Nor are the cases in this report unique; advanced militaries frequently turn to extensive use of firepower when faced with the challenges of fighting highly capable irregular adversaries. Valentino estimated that the Soviets, for instance, were responsible for approximately a million deaths in their occupation of Afghanistan.[6]

As discussed in Chapter 2, there is strong reason to believe that extensive deaths among noncombatants increase recruitment among insurgents and ultimately prolong such wars. Precision fires afford advanced militaries the opportunity to employ fires more discriminately, but there are limits to the degree of precision that can be achieved when militants adopt defensive positions in densely populated areas, such as cities.[7] Commanders thus face a difficult balancing act, needing to employ fires sufficient to disrupt and degrade highly capable VNSAs while not politically strengthening the forces they are attempting to combat.

None of this discussion is meant to imply that militaries *cannot* adapt to the combination of conventional and irregular challenges posed by most state-supported VNSAs. Rather, it suggests that, historically, militaries have repeatedly struggled to balance the competing demands of these two types of warfare that become, at least to some extent, fused through the higher level of capabilities that state support can provide to VNSAs. This struggle, in turn, has important strategic implications.

---

[4] Frederik Logevall, *Embers of War: The Fall of an Empire and the Making of America's Vietnam*, New York: Random House, 2012.

[5] Benjamin A. Valentino, *Final Solutions: Mass Killing and Genocide in the 20th Century*, Ithaca, N.Y.: Cornell University Press, 2004, p. 87.

[6] Valentino, 2004, p. 87.

[7] Amos C. Fox, "Precision Fires Hindered by Urban Jungle," Association of the United States Army, April 16, 2018.

Strategic Challenges

At the strategic level, highly capable state-supported VNSAs present three challenges to the United States' ability to support allies and partners in wars against these hybrid threats.

Viability of Relying on Partners

First, as the case studies in this report suggest, state support for militants can cast doubt on the viability of the OIR model, at least for the more challenging cases. State-supported VNSAs were able to inflict heavy costs on even highly capable militaries, such as the French in the First Indochina War. Many examples from beyond our case studies reinforce this finding, including the heavy losses that the mujahideen inflicted on the Soviets in Afghanistan and Lebanese Hezbollah's initial successes against the IDF. If even advanced militaries such as these struggled against state-supported VNSAs, it calls into question whether less-sophisticated U.S. allies and partners could hope to achieve at least minimally acceptable outcomes against highly capable militants, even with the United States providing a small advisory presence and standoff fires.

This assessment is not meant to imply that state-supported VNSAs are invincible. The cases of conflict examined in this report were selected to represent particularly successful VNSA campaigns as a means of testing the types of most-challenging contingencies for which the United States might need to be prepared. Some U.S. allies and partners may not make the same mistakes that the governments in these case studies made, and many VNSAs will not enjoy the level of cohesion and commitment represented by the Vietminh and Vietcong.

Regarding the first of these points, it is important to acknowledge that many state-backed VNSAs' successes occurred at least in part because of the flaws of their opponents. Hezbollah's initial victories against the IDF, for instance, exploited its adversary's failures in training. When the IDF prepared to fight a large-scale combined-arms fight, it enjoyed considerably more success.[8] Similarly, the United States was able to repulse attacks

---

[8]   Johnson, 2010; Johnson; 2011.

by the Vietcong; it was the commitment of large numbers of NVA forces that ultimately defeated the Saigon regime.[9] But most of the counterinsurgents examined in this study represented at least fairly capable militaries, and many were quite capable. Many U.S. allies and partners will not be able to achieve this degree of military capability through U.S. training and support, at least in a policy-relevant time frame, suggesting that they may be vulnerable without more direct U.S. intervention.

It is also important to acknowledge the wide variation in capabilities among insurgents and other VNSAs. Relatively few will be as cohesive and committed as the Vietminh and Vietcong. Although external powers can help to develop VNSAs' military capabilities, it is much more difficult to develop the organization, leadership, and popular support that characterizes the most successful VNSAs. The 2014–2022 Donbas War is instructive in this regard. Even without the military sophistication of the IDF or the U.S. military, Ukrainian government forces were able to gain the upper hand in fighting against the RLSF, prompting more-direct intervention by Russia. In this case, the insurgency that Russia was supporting was largely an artificial creation of Russia itself. Had Moscow been able to tap into much broader popular support for a violent uprising, it is not clear that the Ukrainian government would have enjoyed as much military success as it did during this period. This example suggests that proxy warfare, although a powerful tool of strategic competition, is still limited by the social and organizational strength of local actors.

Fighting for Time

The case studies in this report suggest that state-supported VNSAs make it particularly difficult for foreign interveners to commit to long-term, direct interventions because of their ability to inflict relatively high levels of casualties on foreign forces, thus taxing the resources of foreign interveners and undermining domestic political support for the war. This dynamic is particularly problematic when the state backers of VNSAs are able to keep their own costs low, as is often the case when they are primarily providing materiel and technical support rather than engaging in fighting directly.

---

[9] Summers, 1995.

Ultimately, of course, the United States lost in Vietnam not because of military defeat but because of a loss of domestic political commitment. Similarly, France may have fared better militarily in its own war in Vietnam if its resources had not been stretched among multiple colonial commitments. But the military capabilities of the Vietcong and Vietminh were an important part of why the United States was not able to sustain its political commitment and the French found themselves stretched thin. Less-capable insurgents would not have inflicted the same number of casualties on intervening forces, nor would they have demanded the same numbers of foreign forces (totaling in the hundreds of thousands for both France and the United States). At lower force commitments and lower casualty levels, both countries may have been able to sustain their interventions over much longer periods. Of course, it is still not certain and perhaps doubtful that the additional time would have resulted in a Saigon regime that was more capable of governing effectively. But there were indications that South Vietnam was beginning to make progress in its counterinsurgency fight with American advice and assistance.[10] Without the direct incursions of the NVA, the regime may have been able to endure.

As discussed in Chapter 2, high levels of casualties can be particularly difficult to sustain domestically in instances of protracted wars with murky (at least to the public) objectives. The United States has been able to sustain prolonged support for regimes such as those in Baghdad and Kabul when it has kept troop deployments and casualties relatively low. The provision of state support to insurgents throws into doubt the United States' ability to pursue this approach.

Sanctuary and Escalation

A fifth proposition advanced in Chapter 2 suggested that state support for VNSAs may impose strategic limitations on foreign interveners' escalation options. Faced with the prospect of a costly and protracted war, states are often tempted to escalate the conflict, either by raising the intensity

---

[10] See, for instance, Lewis Sorley, *A Better War: The Unexamined Victories and Final Tragedy of America's Last Years in Vietnam*, New York: Houghton Mifflin Harcourt Publishing, 1999.

of attacks against the VNSAs themselves or trying to eliminate VNSAs' state support. The latter option could include attacks on the VNSAs' cross-border supply lines or sanctuaries or punitive attacks on the state sponsors, intended to increase the costs of their support.

The case studies in this report illustrate why state support makes such escalatory options problematic. In the case of the Second Indochina War, the United States resorted to all of these options. But options for escalation may be limited, depending on the relative capabilities of the sponsor. In the case of the Second Indochina War, the United States was deterred from launching ground attacks into North Vietnam by the prospect of direct Chinese involvement similar to the Korean War. In the case of the Donbas War, Kyiv was prevented from achieving military victory by the more direct involvement of Russian troops. Especially when major powers are the ones providing the support to VNSAs, there may be little realistic alternative to a protracted and costly hybrid or irregular conflict.

Chapter 2 advanced five propositions about the challenges that state-supported VNSAs might pose to militaries such as those of the United States. These propositions were derived from a review of the military-professional literature. In many cases, the logic behind those propositions was not fully articulated, and the arguments were advanced on the basis of either single cases or illustrative examples chosen selectively from certain cases. The empirical analysis in this report suggests that these five dynamics related to highly capable state-supported VNSAs, ranging from the tactical to strategic levels of war, do indeed pose serious challenges to militaries such as those of the United States.

Looking Forward

What are the military implications of potential contingencies involving highly capable surrogate forces in the coming years?

First, the increased lethality possessed by many state-supported VNSAs looks likely to continue into the future. The United States developed high levels of tactical proficiency in irregular warfare in Afghanistan and Iraq. But just as U.S. capabilities improved, so have those of potential U.S. adversaries. While most of the damage Iran inflicted on U.S. forces in Iraq came in the form of mines, the 2014–2022 war in the Donbas shows how much more militarily sophisticated VNSAs could potentially become, with access to advanced EW, cyber, ISR, and other capabilities. While it is possible that continued improvements in commercial off-the-shelf technology could greatly enhance VNSA capabilities without state support, thus far, truly high-end military capabilities—meaning not just advanced technology but also the training and sustainment necessary to make effective and consistent use of these technologies—have been the preserve of VNSAs with state backing.

Second, because of their potential for increased lethality, state-supported VNSAs can pose a major challenge for those U.S. allies and partners in which they operate. After the experiences in Iraq and Afghanistan (and Vietnam before them), the United States is likely to remain hesitant to become involved again in large-scale, irregular warfare. But support limited to civil assistance, intelligence, military advising, and standoff fires may not be enough to protect U.S. allies and partners against well-developed insurgencies with high levels of state backing. The VNSAs in our case studies were able to either militarily defeat or at least impose large costs on even quite capable state militaries. Weak and fragile states or those with low-quality militaries are unlikely to fare well against such adversaries.

Third, if U.S. forces become directly involved in such wars, they will require mastery of both conventional and irregular skill sets. With its sophisticated ISR capabilities and air dominance, the United States can make it extremely difficult for VNSAs to mass, which, in turn, makes it extremely difficult for them to launch conventional offensives to seize and hold territory. But through irregular operations and tactics, VNSAs can make large portions of U.S. allies and partners essentially ungovernable. Pushing back against such tactics will require some level of continued proficiency in irregular warfare.

Finally, any direct engagement of the United States with Russian or Chinese surrogates, or possibly with those of a nuclear-armed Iran at some point, holds the potential to pose extreme challenges to U.S. forces. With limits on the extent to which the United States could escalate the conflict (at least at costs it would be willing to bear), the situation may be both protracted and deadly. To the extent that the United States could bolster its allies' and partners' ability to fight with relatively little direct commitment of U.S. forces, it may be able to keep costs manageable. However, keeping U.S. commitments limited to restrain the costs of such conflicts has often been difficult in the past.

None of these implications are meant to suggest that state-supported VNSAs are invincible. State support to VNSAs can potentially create political or diplomatic vulnerabilities that the United States might exploit. The United States might reach a diplomatic agreement with foreign backers of VNSAs to withdraw their support. And state support to VNSAs might provoke political backlash within the VNSAs themselves or others in the conflict state that resent foreign involvement or exploitation. At a purely military level, however, state support for VNSAs appears to create a number of military challenges that the United States should anticipate were it ever to become involved in such a conflict again.

Recommendations for the Army

Countering hybrid warfare of the sort practiced by many state-supported VNSAs requires proficiency in both conventional and irregular warfighting, whether the United States is fighting these forces directly or primarily working by, with, and through local partners. With the current emphasis on regaining readiness for high-intensity, conventional warfare with a peer or near-peer adversary, it is unclear whether DoD and the U.S. Army are currently taking the actions that would be necessary to preserve proficiency in both. As the case studies in this report suggest, state-supported VNSAs can exact a high price on intervening militaries that have not prepared for the unique challenges they pose.

At the level of declared policy, both DoD and the Army are committed to readiness for the full range of contingencies, including the hybrid warfare common in cases of proxy wars. The Irregular Warfare Annex of the 2018 National Defense Strategy declares, "We must not—and will not—repeat the 'boom and bust' cycle that has left the United States underprepared for irregular warfare in both Great Power Competition and conflict."[11] In com-

---

[11] U.S. Department of Defense, "Summary of the Irregular Warfare Annex to the National Defense Strategy," 2020, p. 1.

ments made while he was still Secretary of the Army, former Secretary of Defense Mark Esper declared, "We've got to be able to do it all, but our primary focus, priority No. 1, is preparing for high-intensity conflict. . . . We can do it all. It's just managing the force, managing the risk."[12] Similarly, one former commander of U.S. Army Training and Doctrine Command, General Stephen Townsend, appeared to prioritize hybrid threats in public comments: "The future of war will be a hybrid threat. . . . There'll be everything from tanks and missiles and fighter-bombers down to criminal gangs, terrorists, suicide bombers and guerrilla cells. . . . We're going to have to do all of that, the full spectrum of conflict."[13]

But many observers are skeptical that the U.S. military truly is committed to retaining the irregular warfare expertise that is an essential component of preparedness for hybrid conflicts. Many have pointed out that the Army has a history of turning its back on counterinsurgency to focus on conventional warfare. In an interview, Colonel Joe Collins (ret.), a professor at the National War College, asserted, "We have a bad habit of not being able to stop the pendulum in the middle."[14] Similarly, Colonel John Agoglia warned, "I'm concerned that while the Army says we're not going to [forget the lessons of Iraq and Afghanistan], they're not making the adjustments in our education and our training that ensure that our forces and our junior officers and [noncommissioned officers] see this as not a binary but a continuum which they've got to be prepared to fight in."[15] This skepticism is echoed by many others, who have observed that many training events have eliminated any irregular elements, generating-force institutions focused on irregular warfare have been targeted for budget cuts, and DoD directives that formerly had emphasized the need to balance capabilities between conventional and irregular forms of warfare have now gone silent on the latter.[16]

---

[12] Sydney J. Freedberg Jr., "Army Can Manage Both Mideast & Great Powers: Sec. Esper," *Breaking Defense*, May 20, 2019.

[13] Sean D. Naylor, "After Years of Fighting Insurgencies, the Army Pivots to Training for a Major War," *Yahoo News*, October 30, 2018.

[14] Naylor, 2018.

[15] Naylor, 2018.

[16] Todd South, "The Army Is Shutting Down Its Highly Praised Asymmetric Warfare Group," *Army Times*, October 2, 2020; John Vrolyk, "Insurgency, Not War, Is Chi-

A study such as this one cannot provide detailed guidance on how DoD or the Army should allocate scarce resources across the full range of possible contingencies, and in any case, the services are already examining how they should update the guidance provided in the Irregular Warfare annex of the 2018 U.S. National Defense Strategy. We can, however, suggest a number of measures that DoD and the U.S. Army in particular could undertake to maintain readiness for the sort of threats posed by state-supported VNSAs in proxy conflicts, like those described in this report.

Doctrine

The last major overhaul of U.S. military doctrine for irregular warfare was made with the exigencies of OIF and Operational Enduring Freedom–Afghanistan (OEF-A) in mind. In both cases, the United States was directly engaged in counterinsurgency on a massive scale against relatively low-technology adversaries. Although it is impossible to rule out such contingencies in the future, the range of irregular and hybrid threats posed by state-supported VNSAs is much broader than the circumstances that gave rise to the last overhaul of doctrine in this field. Doctrine should accordingly be updated. Observers have pointed out, for instance, that doctrine has not been updated to reflect the "by, with, and through" approach at the center of OIR and that the United States would employ in future contingencies against state-supported VNSAs, if feasible.[17] Army doctrine for intelligence preparation of the battlefield does not have an intelligence template specific to hybrid contingencies.[18]

Of course, threats do not remain static, so even once the Army and other elements of the Joint Force update their doctrine to reflect current circumstances, they will need to continue to make investments in updating their

---

na's Most Likely Course of Action," *War on the Rocks*, December 19, 2019; Tammy S. Schultz, "Tool of Peace and War: Save the Peacekeeping and Stability Operations Institute," Council on Foreign Relations, July 31, 2018.

[17] Michael X. Garrett, William H. Dunbar, Bryan C. Hilferty, and Robert R. Rodock, "The By-With-Through Approach: An Army Component Perspective," *Joint Force Quarterly*, Vol. 89, 2nd Quarter 2018, p. 55.

[18] Headquarters, Department of the Army, *Intelligence Preparation of the Battlefield*, ATP 2-01.3, 2019, pp. 6-12–6-14.

understanding of evolving threats and appropriate doctrinal responses if they believe that proxy warfare represents a sufficient threat to justify at least modest investments. If the Army wants to maintain its proficiency in such combat, it is vital that the Army continue to resource such entities as the Irregular Warfare Force Modernization Proponent in the Mission Command Center of Excellence at Fort Leavenworth. The Army's dissolution of the Asymmetric Warfare Group at Fort Meade eliminated an important resource for irregular warfare and sent a signal of the Army's willingness to maintain capabilities in this field.

Organization

The demands of combat against sophisticated, state-supported VNSAs may have implications for force structure, force design, and even the extent to which the Army relies on contracted support functions.

When the United States fights irregular or hybrid wars directly, rather than relying almost entirely on local forces, it can impose a great deal of stress on some types of units for which demand is vastly greater than the supply currently in U.S. force structure. These units may include special operations forces, aviation, explosive ordnance disposal, human intelligence specialists and interrogators, military police (especially law and order detachments), and so on. It would be impractical to maintain these forces on a scale adequate to meet the sort of demand posed by OIF and OEF-A at the height of these operations. On the other hand, most of these unit types are particularly "rank-heavy" (i.e., have a disproportionately large number of more-experienced personnel), meaning that new units cannot be "grown" quickly as demand requires (at least not without sacrificing considerable quality). It is beyond the scope of this study to determine what the right mix of forces is across the varied demands of conventional, hybrid, and irregular warfare. It is important for the Army and the Joint Force, however, to not lose sight of the potential demands for these types of forces even as the current focus is on high-intensity warfighting.[19]

Hybrid warfare can also pose particular challenges to existing Army unit structures, whether the United States is fighting directly or primarily

---

[19] Watts, Polich, and Eaton, 2015.

through partnered operations. It demands the close integration of air and ground capabilities required in conventional warfare against sophisticated adversaries. But because hybrid warfare tends to be more dispersed than conventional combat, involving lower-echelon units fighting across large areas, it may be necessary to push capabilities for air-ground combat integration to lower echelons.[20] Partnered operations pose different challenges to force design, since doctrinal units are commonly broken apart and used in nondoctrinal ways in partnered operations.[21] Neither of these challenges (or potentially others posed by hybrid warfare) necessarily dictate changes to force design. But the Army may need to at least develop mechanisms to facilitate rapid adaptation of doctrinal units.

It is also important to think about demand in broader terms than only uniformed military personnel. A large proportion of personnel demands during OIF, OEF-A, and even OIR were met by contractors. But in the more hazardous environments common in wars against state-supported VNSAs, the United States may not be able to rely on meeting so many of its demands from outside the uniformed military. The Mosul Study Group, for instance, recently concluded that "[t]he U.S. Army may be reaching the limits of its approach to contractor support and utilization . . . [and] must re-examine the employment of contractors in a high intensity conflict."[22]

Training

Training should similarly be adapted for contingencies involving militarily sophisticated VNSAs. Ever-larger numbers of military officers will go through their professional development with little if any direct exposure to irregular or hybrid warfare. Unless leaders are forced to prepare for these sorts of contingencies—especially by making them a part of capstone training events such as Combat Training Center exercises—they risk losing familiarity with the broader spectrum of military operations. Although the Army has training templates for hybrid opponents, some observers fear that

---

[20] Johnson, 2011.

[21] Garrett et al., 2018.

[22] Mosul Study Group, *What the Battle for Mosul Teaches the Force*, Fort Leavenworth, Kan.: Department of the Army, TRADOC, 2017, p. 28.

it is already focused exclusively on high-intensity, conventional warfare.[23] To better focus on hybrid contingencies, training events might involve a greater emphasis on the nondoctrinal ways in which soldiers are frequently employed in partnered operations.[24] They might also integrate Air Force personnel to attempt to replicate the intensive collaboration between air and ground capabilities required for hybrid warfare.[25] Such training will be required whether the United States is engaged in combat directly or simply advising partners on how to conduct operations.

Leader Development and Education

Given the complexity of hybrid warfare, leaders must be able to adapt quickly to a wide variety of demands to succeed at acceptable cost. If DoD and the Army choose to prepare leaders for these challenges and promote an adaptable mindset, it is critical that professional military education remain broad-based, including courses focused on irregular and hybrid warfare and military operations among local populations.[26] To prevent an exclusive focus on conventional warfare, military schoolhouses might make one or more of such courses mandatory or otherwise incentivize students to ensure that their education prepares them for the full spectrum of military operations.

Of course, leader development does not occur solely in the classroom. Practical experience is critical for developing the range of skills that leaders will require to thrive in hybrid environments. DoD's current focus on the competition space short of armed conflict has the potential to provide such experiences to emerging leaders, but only if the Army (and other ser-

---

[23] Naylor, 2018. Similar observations have been made about the Marine Corps; see, for instance, Vrolyk, 2019. For the current U.S. Army training template for hybrid contingencies, see U.S. Training and Doctrine Command (TRADOC), *Hybrid Threat*, TC 7-100, Washington, D.C.: Headquarters Department of the Army, 2010.

[24] Garrett et al., 2018.

[25] Johnson, 2011.

[26] Of course, such advice is more easily offered than enacted—as suggested by the frequency with which this recommendation has been made. See Johnson et al., 2019; and Watts, Polich, and Eaton, 2015.

vices) manage such opportunities correctly. In the past, for instance, many advisory assignments were viewed as not "career-enhancing." The Security Force Assistance Brigades are one high-profile initiative that might serve as a litmus test for the Army's commitment to preparing for the full spectrum of operations, including "by, with, and through" operations to counter irregular or hybrid threats. If the Security Force Assistance Brigades are disbanded (without an appropriate alternative), or if the leaders of these brigades are not selected for promotion and key assignments at the same rate as officers focused on high-intensity, conventional warfare, it will send a strong signal.[27]

Personnel

Military operations conducted among civilian populations inevitably benefit from knowledge of the local society. Developing regional expertise broadly within the military, however, is exceptionally difficult, given the high technical demands of conducting modern warfare. There are positions within the U.S. military and especially the U.S. Army, however, that do cultivate such regional expertise, particularly Foreign Affairs Officers and some intelligence specialists. The Army and other services could expand the number of such billets, with a focus on the allies and partners identified as potentially vulnerable in the previous section. Alternatively, given resource constraints, the Army could reallocate its existing level of personnel to focus more heavily on these at-risk countries.

---

[27] Naylor, 2018.

Abbreviations

AFU	Armed Forces of Ukraine
ATGM	antitank guided missile
C2	command and control
CCP	Chinese Communist Party
DNR	Donetsk People's Republic
DoD	U.S. Department of Defense
EU	European Union
EW	electronic warfare
GCC	Gulf Cooperation Council
IED	improvised explosive device
ISR	intelligence, surveillance, and reconnaissance
LNR	Luhansk People's Republic
MBT	main battle tank
MRDC	Missile Research and Development Center
NATO	North Atlantic Treaty Organization
NLF	National Liberation Front
NVA	North Vietnamese Army
OEF-A	Operational Enduring Freedom–Afghanistan
OIF	Operation Iraqi Freedom
OIR	Operation Inherent Resolve

PLA	People's Liberation Army
RLSF	Russian-led separatist forces
RPD	Ruchnoy Pulemyot Degtyaryova
SAM	surface-to-air missile
TTP	tactics, techniques, and procedures
UAE	United Arab Emirates
UAS	unmanned aircraft system
UAV	unmanned aerial vehicle
USS	United States Ship
VNSA	violent nonstate actor
WBIED	water-borne improvised explosive device

References

"Al Houthi: The Assassination of Salih Is a 'Historic' Day: We Took Down the Conspiracy in 3 Days [Al-Houthi: Ightial Salih Yawm Tarikhi . . . Asqatna Al-Mu'amara fi 3 Ayam]," *Annahar*, December 4, 2017.

Almeida, Alex, Jeremy Vaughan, and Michael Knights, "Houthi Antishipping Attacks in the Bab al-Mandab Strait," The Washington Institute, October 6, 2016.

Altman, Howard, "Lessons for the US Military from the Russian Invasion of Ukraine," *Military Times*, March 6, 2020.

"Anatomy of a 'Drone Boat,'" *Conflict Armament Research*, December 2017.

Anderson, Noel, "Competitive Intervention and Its Consequences for Civil Wars," Ph.D. thesis, Massachusetts Institute of Technology, 2016.

"Armed Drones Are a Growing Threat from Rebels in Yemen," *Wall Street Journal Video*, May 2, 2019.

Athey, Philip, "Thousands of Marines with 26th MEU Move into the Red Sea," *Marine Corps Times*, January 13, 2020.

Aydin, Aysegul, and Patrick M. Regan, "Networks of Third-Party Interveners and Civil War Duration," *European Journal of International Relations*, Vol. 18, No. 3, 2011, pp. 573–597.

Babbitt, Eileen, "Self-Determination as a Component of Conflict Intractability: Implications for Negotiation," in Hurst Hannum and Eileen Babbit, eds., *Negotiating Self-Determination*, Lanham, Md.: Lexington Books, 2006, pp. 115–118.

Baczynska, Gabriela, and Aleksandar Vasovik, "Pushing Locals Aside, Russians Take Top Rebel Posts in East Ukraine," Reuters, July 27, 2014.

Baker, W. R., "The Easter Offensive of 1972: A Failure to Use Intelligence," originally in *Military Intelligence Professional Bulletin*, 1998, reprinted in *Small Wars Journal*, January 26, 2016, As of April 3, 2020:
https://smallwarsjournal.com/jrnl/art/
the-easter-offensive-of-1972-a-failure-to-use-intelligence

Balcells, Laia, and Stathis N. Kalyvas, "Does Warfare Matter? Severity, Duration, and Outcomes of Civil Wars," *Journal of Conflict Resolution*, 2014.

Balmforth, Tom, "A Guide to the Separatists of Eastern Ukraine," Radio Free Europe–Radio Liberty, June 3, 2014.

Barbashin, Anton, and Hannah Thoburn, "Putin's Brain: Alexander Dugin and the Philosophy Behind Putin's Invasion of Crimea," *Foreign Affairs*, March 31, 2014.

"The Battle of Ilovaisk: Mapping Russian Military Presence in Eastern Ukraine, August-September 2014," Forensic Architecture Project, undated. As of April 20, 2020:
https://ilovaisk.forensic-architecture.org

Beckhusen, Robert, "The Yemeni Air Force Probably No Longer Exists," *War Is Boring*, March 27, 2015.

Binnie, Jeremy, "Iran Rolls Out Another Medium-Range SAM," *Jane's*, November 12, 2013.

Borgen, Christopher, "Law, Rhetoric, Strategy: Russia and Self-Determination Before and After Crimea," *International Law Studies*, Vol. 91, No. 216, 2015, pp. 265–267.

Boucek, Christopher, "War in Saada: From Local Insurrection to National Challenge," Carnegie Endowment, April 2010.

Bowers, Christopher O., "Identifying Emerging Hybrid Adversaries," *Parameters*, Spring 2012, pp. 39–50.

Bradley, Mark Philip, *Vietnam at War*, New York: Oxford University Press, 2009.

Brown, Daniel, "The Pentagon Showed Off These Weapons That Iran Has Given to the Taliban and Houthis, Saying It Wasn't a Political Stunt," *Business Insider*, November 30, 2018.

Browning, Noah, and Sami Aboudi, "Former President Saleh Dead After Switching Sides in Yemen's Civil War," Reuters, December 4, 2017.

Brunson, Jonathan, "Implementing the Minsk Agreements Might Drive Ukraine to Civil War. That's Been Russia's Plan All Along," *War on the Rocks*, February 1, 2019.

Bugayova, Nataliya, "How We Got Here with Russia: The Kremlin's Worldview," Institute for the Study of War, March 2019.

Bugayova, Nataliya, Mason Clark, and George Barros, "Putin Accelerates Ukraine Campaign Amid Converging Crises," *Russia in Review*, March 24, 2020.

Bukkvoll, Tor, "Russian Special Operations Forces in Crimea and Donbas," *Parameters*, Carlisle Barracks, Vol. 46, No. 2, Summer 2016.

Cable, James, *The Geneva Conference of 1954 on Indochina*, New York: Springer, 1986.

Case, Sean, and Klement Anders, "Putin's Undeclared War: Summer 2014 Russian Artillery Strikes Against Ukraine," *Bellingcat*, December 21, 2016.

Cech, Adam, and Jakub Janda, "Caught in the Act: Proof of Russian Military Intervention in Ukraine," Wilfried Martens Centre for European Studies, July 2015.

"CENTCOM: MQ-9 Reaper Shot Down Over Yemen Last Week," *Military Times*, June 16, 2019.

Collins, Liam, and Harrison Morgan, "King of Battle: Russia Breaks Out the Big Guns," Association of the United States Army, January 22, 2019.

Connable, Ben, and Martin C. Libicki, *How Insurgencies End*, Santa Monica, Calif.: RAND Corporation, MG-965-MCIA, 2010. As of January 23, 2023: https://www.rand.org/pubs/monographs/MG965.html

Connell, Mary Ellen, and Ryan Evans, "Russia's Ambiguous Warfare and Implications for the U.S. Marine Corps," *MCU Journal*, Vol. 7, No. 1, Spring 2016, pp. 30–45.

Cooper, Helene, Thomas Gibbons-Neff, and Eric Schmitt, "Army Special Forces Secretly Help Saudis Combat Threat from Yemen Rebels," *New York Times*, May 3, 2018.

Cooper, Tom, "The Houthis' Do-It-Yourself Air Defenses: Part Two," *War Is Boring*, January 16, 2018a.

Cooper, Tom, "The Houthis' Do-It-Yourself Air Defenses: Part Three," *War Is Boring*, January 23, 2018b.

Copp, Tara, "Aegis Defense System Helped Stop Missile Attack on USS Mason," *Stars and Stripes*, October 13, 2016.

Czuperski, Maksymilian, John Herbst, Eliot Higgins, Alina Polyakova, Damon Wilson, "Hiding in Plain Sight: Russia's War in Ukraine," The Atlantic Council, October 15, 2015, p. 8.

Darczewska, Jolanta, *The Anatomy of Russian Information Warfare, the Crimean Operation, a Case Study,* Warsaw, Poland: Centre for Eastern Studies, May 2014.

Al-Dawsari, Nadwa, "Running Around in Circles: How Saudi Arabia Is Losing Its War in Yemen to Iran," Middle East Institute, March 3, 2020.

Deni, John, "Tie Lethal Aid for Ukraine to an Admission That NATO Made a Mistake," *War on the Rocks*, December 22, 2017.

Deutsch, Karl W., "External Involvement in Internal War," in Harry Eckstein, ed., *Internal War: Problems and Approaches*, New York: Free Press of Glencoe, 1964.

DeYoung, Karen, "U.S. Releases Images It Says Show Russia Has Fired Artillery Over Border into Ukraine," *Washington Post*, July 27, 2014.

Al-Din, Maysaa Shuja, "Federalism in Yemen: A Catalyst for War, the Present Reality, and the Inevitable Future," Sanaa Center for Strategic Studies, February 2019.

Al-Din, Maysaa Shuja, "Iran and Houthis: Between Political Alliances and Sectarian Tensions," Al-Masdar Online, June 15, 2017.

"Dispatch from the Field: Mines and IEDs Employed by Houthi Forces on Yemen's West Coast," *Conflict Armament Research*, September 2018.

DoD—*See* U.S. Department of Defense.

Dorell, Oren, "Analysis: Ukraine Forces Outmanned, Outgunned by Rebels," *USA Today*, February 23, 2015.

"Evolution of UAVs Employed by Houthi Forces in Yemen," *Conflict Armament Research*, February 2020.

Fahim, Kareem, "Houthi Rebels Kill 45 U.A.E. Soldiers in Yemen Fighting," *New York Times*, September 4, 2015.

Fall, Bernard B., "The Political-Religious Sects of Vietnam," *Pacific Affairs*, Vol. 28, No. 3, September 1955, pp. 235–253.

Fearon, James D., and David D. Laitin, "Ethnicity, Insurgency, and Civil War," *American Political Science Review*, Vol. 97, No. 1, 2003, pp. 75–90.

Feierstein, Gerald, "Congressional Testimony Before the House Foreign Affairs Subcommittee on the Middle East and North Africa," April 14, 2015.

Ferguson, Jonathan, and N.R. Jenzen-Jones, *Raising Red Flags: An Examination of Arms & Munitions in the Ongoing Conflict in Ukraine, 2014*, Australia: Armament Research Services (ARES), November 18, 2014.

Fitch, Asa, "How Yemen's Houthis Are Ramping Up Their Weapons Capability; Saudi Forces Have Intercepted More Than 100 Missiles Since 2015," *Wall Street Journal*, April 25, 2018.

Fox, Amos C., "Precision Fires Hindered by Urban Jungle," Association of the United States Army, April 16, 2018.

Fox, Roger P., *Air Base Defense in the Republic of Vietnam, 1961–1973*, Washington, D.C.: Office of Air Force History, 1979.

Freedberg, Jr., Sydney J., "Army Can Manage Both Mideast & Great Powers: Sec. Esper," *Breaking Defense*, May 20, 2019.

Freedman, Lawrence, "Ukraine and the Art of Exhaustion," *War on the Rocks*, August 11, 2015.

Galeotti, Mark, "The 'Gerasimov Doctrine' and Russian Non-Linear War," *In Moscow's Shadows*, July 6, 2014.

Galeotti, Mark, "The Mythical 'Gerasimov Doctrine' and the Language of Threat," *Critical Studies on Security*, Vol. 7, No. 2, 2019, pp. 157–161.

Garrett, Michael X., William H. Dunbar, Bryan C. Hilferty, and Robert R. Rodock, "The By-With-Through Approach: An Army Component Perspective," *Joint Force Quarterly*, Vol. 89, 2nd Quarter 2018, p. 55.

Gazula, Mohan, "Cyber Warfare Conflict Analysis and Case Studies," Massachusetts Institute of Technology, Working Paper CISL# 2017-10, May 2017.

Gelpi, Christopher, Peter D. Feaver, and Jason Reifler. "Success Matters: Casualty Sensitivity and the War in Iraq," *International Security*, Vol. 30, No. 3, December 2005, pp. 7–46.

Gibbons, William C., *The U.S. Government and the Vietnam War*, Princeton, N.J.: Princeton University Press, 1995.

Giles, Keir, "Handbook of Russian Information Warfare," Research Division, NATO Defense College, November 2016.

Glenn, Russell W., *All Glory Is Fleeting: Insights from the Second Lebanon War*, Santa Monica, Calif.: RAND Corporation, MG-708-1-JFCOM, 2012. As of November 10, 2022:
https://www.rand.org/pubs/monographs/MG708-1.html

Greenberg, Andy, "The Untold Story of NotPetya, the Most Destructive Cyberattack in History," *Wired*, August 22, 2018.

Grytsenko, Oksana, "Thousands of Russian Soldiers Fought at Ilovaisk, Around a Hundred Were Killed," *Kyiv Post*, April 6, 2018.

Al-Haj, Ahmed, "Fighting Sharply Rises in Yemen, Endangering Peace Efforts," Associated Press, January 29, 2020.

Hammel, Eric, *Fire in the Streets: The Battle for Hue: Tet, 1968*, Pacifica, Calif.: Pacifica Press, 1991.

Hammes, Thomas X., *The Sling and the Stone: On War in the 21st Century*, St. Paul, Minn.: Zenith Press, 2006.

Headquarters, Department of the Army, *Intelligence Preparation of the Battlefield*, Washington, D.C.: Department of the Army, ATP 2-01.3, 2019.

Himmiche, Ahmed, Dakshinie Ruwanthika Gunaratne, Gregory Johnsen, and Adrian Wilkinson, "Letter Dated 27 January 2017 from the Panel of Experts on Yemen Addressed to the President of the Security Council," United Nations Security Council, January 31, 2017.

Himmiche, Ahmed, Fernando Rosenfeld Carvajal, Dakshinie Ruwanthika Gunaratne, Gregory Johnsen, and Adrian Wilkinson, "Letter Dated 26 January 2018 from the Panel of Experts on Yemen Mandated by Security Council Resolution 2342 (2017) Addressed to the President of the Security Council," United Nations Security Council, January 26, 2018.

Himmiche, Ahmed, Fernando Rosenfeld Carvajal, Wolf-Christian Paes, Henry Thompson, and Marie-Louise Tongas, "Letter Dated 25 January 2019 from the Panel of Experts on Yemen Addressed to the President of the Security Council," United Nations Security Council, January 29, 2019.

Hoffman, Frank G., "'Hybrid' vs. Compound War: The Janus Choice," *Armed Forces Journal International*, October 2009.

Hoffman, Frank G., "Hybrid Warfare and Challenges," *Joint Force Quarterly*, Vol. 52, No. 1, 2009, pp. 34–48.

Holcomb, Franklin, "The Kremlin's Irregular Army: Ukrainian Separatist Order of Battle," Institute for the Study of War, *Russian and Ukraine Security Report No. 3*, September 2017.

Hook, Brian, "Iran Regime's Transfer of Arms to Proxy Groups & On," U.S. Department of State, YouTube, November 29, 2018.

"Houthi Drone Attacks on 2 Saudi Aramco Oil Facilities Spark Fires," *Al Jazeera*, September 14, 2019.

"Houthi Naval Mine Reportedly Kills Three Egyptian Fshermen in Red Sea," Almasdar Online, March 24, 2020.

"Houthi Rebel Drone Kills Several at Saudi Coalition Parade," *France 24*, October 1, 2019.

"The Houthis: The Military Reality and Sources of Support [Al-Huthiyun: Al-Haqiqa Al-ʿAskriya wa Masadir Al-Daʿm]," Strategic Fiker Center for Studies, May 18, 2015.

Hubbard, Ben, "Saudi Death Sentences in Khashoggi Killing Fail to Dispel Questions," *New York Times*, December 23, 2019.

Human Rights Council, "Situation of Human Rights in Yemen, Including Violations and Abuses Since September 2014," September 2019.

Hunt, David, *Vietnam's Southern Revolution: From Peasant Insurrection to Total War*, Amherst, Mass.: University of Massachusetts Press, 2008.

International Crisis Group, "Ukraine: The Line," Briefing No. 81, July 18, 2016.

International Crisis Group, "Rebels Without a Cause: Russia's Proxies in Eastern Ukraine," *Report No. 254*, July 16, 2019.

"Iranian Technology Transfers to Yemen," *Conflict Armament Research*, March 2017.

Jane's/IHS, "Ukraine: Air Force," last updated July 5, 2019. As of April 20, 2020:
https://janes.ihs.com/Janes/Display/1319142

Jane's/IHS, "Ukraine: Army," last updated February 12, 2020. As of April 20, 2020:
https://janes.ihs.com/Janes/Display/ukras010-cis

Jane's/IHS, "Ukraine: Executive Summary," last updated March 23, 2020. As of April 20, 2020:
https://janes.ihs.com/Janes/Display/ukras010-cis

Jarabik, Balazs, "Escalation in Donbas: Ukraine Fights for the Status Quo," *War on the Rocks*, February 8, 2017.

Jentleson, Bruce W., and Rebecca L. Britton, "Still Pretty Prudent: Post-Cold War American Public Opinion on the Use of Military Force," *Journal of Conflict Resolution*, Vol. 42, No. 4, August 1998, pp. 395–417.

Johnson, David E., *Military Capabilities for Hybrid War: Insights from the Israel Defense Forces in Lebanon and Gaza*, Santa Monica, Calif.: RAND Corporation, OP-285-A, 2010. As of November 9, 2022:
https://www.rand.org/pubs/occasional_papers/OP285.html

Johnson, David E., *Hard Fighting: Israel in Lebanon and Gaza*, Santa Monica, Calif.: RAND Corporation, MG-1085-A/AF, 2011a. As of November 9, 2022:
https://www.rand.org/pubs/monographs/MG1085.html

Johnson, David E., *Heavy Armor in the Future Security Environment*, Santa Monica, Calif.: RAND Corporation, OP-334-A, 2011b. As of November 2, 2022:
https://www.rand.org/pubs/occasional_papers/OP334.html

Johnson, David E., Agnes Gereben Schaefer, Brenna Allen, Raphael S. Cohen, Gian Gentile, James Hoobler, Michael Schwille, Jerry M. Sollinger, and Sean M. Zeigler, *The U.S. Army and the Battle for Baghdad: Lessons Learned—And Still to Be Learned*, Santa Monica, Calif.: RAND Corporation, RR-3076-A, 2019. As of November 10, 2022:
https://www.rand.org/pubs/research_reports/RR3076.html

Joint Chiefs of Staff, *Joint Operations*, Joint Publication (JP) 3-0, October 22, 2018.

Kagan, Frederick, Nataliya Bugayova, and Jennifer Cafarella, "Confronting the Russian Challenge: A New Approach for the U.S.," Institute for the Study of War, June 2019.

Kalyvas, Stathis N., and Laia Balcells, "International System and Technologies of Rebellion: How the End of the Cold War Shaped Internal Conflict," *American Political Science Review*, Vol. 104, No. 3, August 2010, pp. 415–429.

"'Kamikaze' Drones Used by Houthi Forces to Attack Coalition Missile Defence Systems," *Conflict Armament Research*, March 2017.

Karam, Robert, "Testimony to Senate Foreign Relations Committee from Former Assistant Secretary of Defense for International Security Affairs: U.S. Policy Towards Yemen," video, C-Span, April 17, 2018.

Karsten, Joshua, "Houthi Rebels in Yemen Claim to Shoot Down US Drone," *Stars and Stripes*, August 21, 2019.

Kavanagh, Jennifer, Bryan Frederick, Matthew Povlock, Stacie L. Pettyjohn, Angela O'Mahony, Stephen Watts, Nathan Chandler, John Speed Meyers, and Eugeniu Han, *The Past, Present, and Future of U.S. Ground Interventions: Identifying Trends, Characteristics, and Signposts*, Santa Monica, Calif.: RAND Corporation, RR-1831-A, 2017. As of January 23, 2023: https://www.rand.org/pubs/research_reports/RR1831.html

Kendall, Bridget, "Crimea Crisis: Russian President Putin's Speech Annotated," BBC News, March 19, 2014.

Khan, Umer, "'New Generation Urban Battlespace': The Development of Russian Military Thinking and Capabilities in Urban Warfare Since the Cold War, 1991–2019," PhD dissertation, University of Buckingham, January 2020.

Kivimaki, Veli-Pekka, "Tankspotting: How to Identify the T072B3," *Bellingcat*, May 28, 2015.

Knights, Michael, "The Houthi War Machine: From Guerrilla War to State Capture," *CTC Sentinel*, September 2018.

Kocher, Matthew Adam, Thomas B. Pepinsky, and Stathis N. Kalyvas, "Aerial Bombing and Counterinsurgency in the Vietnam War," *American Journal of Political Science*, Vol. 55, No. 2, April 2011, pp. 201–218.

Kofman, Michael, Katya Migacheva, Brian Nichiporuk, Andrew Radin, Olesya Tkacheva, and Jenny Oberholtzer, *Lessons from Russia's Operations in Crimea and Eastern Ukraine*, Santa Monica, Calif.: RAND Corporation, RR-1498-A, 2017. As of November 9, 2022: https://www.rand.org/pubs/research_reports/RR1498.html

Kononczuk, Wojciech, "Ukraine Withdraws from Signing the Association Agreement in Vilnius: The Motives and Implications," Warsaw, Poland: Centre for Eastern Studies (Osrodek Studiow Wschodnich), November 27, 2013.

Kopets, Keith F., "The Combined Action Program: Vietnam," *Military Review*, July–August 2002, pp. 79–80.

Kopp, Carlo, "Are Helicopters Vulnerable?" *Australian Aviation*, March 2005.

Kowalewski, Annie, "Disinformation and Reflexive Control: The New Cold War," *Georgetown Security Studies Review*, February 1, 2017.

Krepinevich, Jr., Andrew F., *The Army and Vietnam*, Baltimore, Md.: Johns Hopkins University Press, 1986.

Lanning, Michael Lee, and Dan Cragg, *Inside the VC and the NVA*, New York: Fawcett Columbine, 1992.

Lehrke, Dylan Lee, Miko Vranic, and Reed Foster, "Cold War II? Understanding the Balance of Power and Proxy Wars Between NATO and Russia," *Jane's Intelligence Briefing*, August 8, 2019.

Le Mon, Christopher J., "Moving from Partisan to Peacemaker in Yemen," in Andrew Miller and Dafna Rand, eds., *Reengaging the Middle East*, Washington, D.C.: Brookings, 2020.

Locks, Benjamin, "Bad Guys Know What Works: Asymmetric Warfare and the Third Offset," *War on the Rocks*, June 23, 2015.

Logevall, Frederik, *Embers of War: The Fall of an Empire and the Making of America's Vietnam*, New York: Random House, 2012.

"A Long Fight Ahead: The Army Is Gaining the Upper Hand in Yemen's Civil War: Still, No End Is Near," *The Economist*, January 4, 2018.

Lyall, Jason, Graeme Blair, and Kosuke Imai, "Explaining Support for Combatants During Wartime: A Survey Experiment in Afghanistan," *American Political Science Review*, Vol. 107, No. 4, November 2013, pp. 679–705.

Lyall, Jason, and Isaiah Wilson, III, "Rage Against the Machines: Explaining Outcomes in Counterinsurgency Wars," *International Organization*, Vol. 63, No. 1, Winter 2009, pp. 67–106.

Mansour, Renad, and Peter Salisbury, "Between Order and Chaos: A New Approach to Stalled State Transformations in Iraq and Yemen," *Chatham House*, September 2019.

"'Maskirovka' Is Russian Secret War: Sneaky Tactics Are an Old Russian Tradition," *War Is Boring*, August 26, 2014.

Masuhr, Niklas, "Lessons of the War in Ukraine for Western Military Strategy," *CSS Analyses in Security Policy*, No. 242, April 2019.

Mazzetti, Mark, and David D. Kirkpatrick, "Saudi Arabia Leads Air Assault in Yemen," *New York Times*, March 25, 2015.

McCuen, John J., "Hybrid Wars," *Military Review*, March–April 2008, p. 109.

Mezzofiore, Gianluca, "Igor Strelkov: I Started War in Eastern Ukraine," *International Business Times*, November 21, 2014.

"MH17 Missile 'Came from Russia', Dutch-Led Investigators Say," BBC News, September 28, 2016.

Miller, Christopher, "Anxious Ukraine Risks Escalation in 'Creeping Offensive,'" Radio Free Europe–Radio Liberty, January 30, 2017.

"Mines and IEDs Employed by Houthi Forces on Yemen's West Coast," *Conflict Armament Research*, September 2018.

Ministry of Foreign Affairs of Ukraine, "10 Facts You Should Know About Russian Military Aggression Against Ukraine," December 19, 2019.

Missile Defense Project, "Interactive: The Missile War in Yemen," Missile Threat, Center for Strategic and International Studies, December 10, 2019.

Moore, Matthew, "Selling to Both Sides: The Effects of Major Conventional Weapons Transfers on Civil War Severity and Duration," *International Interactions*, Vol. 38, No. 3, 2012, pp. 325–347.

Mosul Study Group, *What the Battle for Mosul Teaches the Force*, Fort Leavenworth, Kan.: Department of the Army, TRADOC, 2017, p. 28.

Muhsin, Dhia, "Houthi Use of Drones Delivers Potent Message in Yemen War," *IISS Blog*, August 27, 2019.

al-Mujahed, Ali, and Hugh Laylor, "Saudi-Led Airstrikes Intensify in Yemen as Possible Coalition Land Attack Looms," *Washington Post*, March 28, 2015.

Mukhashaf, Mohammed, "Yemen Houthi Fighters Backed by Tanks Reach Central Aden," Reuters, April 1, 2015.

Mumford, Andrew, *Proxy Warfare*, Cambridge, UK: Polity, 2013.

Nadimi, Farzin, "Iran Develops Air Defense Capability for Possible Regional Role," The Washington Institute, August 27, 2019.

Nadimi, Farzin, and Michael Knights, "Iran's Support to Houthi Air Defenses in Yemen," The Washington Institute, April 4, 2018.

"Naval Mine Kills Yemeni Coastguards in Bab al-Mandeb," *Al Arabiya English*, March 11, 2017.

Naylor, Sean D., "After Years of Fighting Insurgencies, the Army Pivots to Training for a Major War," *Yahoo News*, October 30, 2018.

"New Houthi Weapon Emerges: A Drone Boat," *Defense News*, February 19, 2017.

Nissenbaum, Dion, Summer Said, and Nancy A. Youssef, "Suspicions Rise That Saudi Oil Attack Came from Outside Yemen," *Wall Street Journal*, September 14, 2019.

Pamuk, Humeyra, "Exclusive: U.S. Probe of Saudi Oil Attack Shows It Came from North—Report," Reuters, December 19, 2019.

Parfitt, Tom, "Russian Tanks, Troops 'Decisive in Eastern Ukraine Battles,'" *Chicagorazom*, March 31, 2015.

Paul, Christopher, Colin P. Clarke, and Beth Grill, *Victory Has a Thousand Fathers: Sources of Success in Counterinsurgency*, Santa Monica, Calif.: RAND Corporation, MG-964-OSD, 2010. As of November 9, 2022: https://www.rand.org/pubs/monographs/MG964.html

Paul, Christopher, Colin P. Clarke, Beth Grill, and Molly Dunigan, *Paths to Victory: Lessons from Modern Insurgencies*, Santa Monica, Calif.: RAND Corporation, RR-291/1-OSD, 2013. As of November 9, 2022: https://www.rand.org/pubs/research_reports/RR291z1.html

Pawlyk, Oriana, "Sanctions Are Impacting Russia's Electronic Warfare Campaign in Ukraine, Officials Claim," Military.com, October 30, 2019.

Payne, Keith B., and John S. Foster, "Russian Strategy: Expansion, Crisis, and Conflict," *Comparative Strategy*, Vol. 36, No. 1, 2017.

Qiang Zhai, *China and the Vietnam Wars*, Chapel Hill, N.C.: University of North Carolina Press, 2000.

Randolph, Stephen P., *Powerful and Brutal Weapons: Nixon, Kissinger, and the Easter Offensive*, Cambridge, Mass.: Harvard University Press, 2007.

Record, Jeffrey, "External Assistance: Enabler of Insurgent Success, *Parameters*, Autumn 2006, pp. 36–49.

Rempfer, Kyle, "Iran Killed More U.S. Troops in Iraq Than Previously Known, Pentagon Says," *Military Times*, April 4, 2019.

Roblin, Sébastien, "The Largest-Caliber Mortar System in the World Is Shelling Cities in Syria and Ukraine," *Offiziere.ch*, April 25, 2016a.

Roblin, Sébastien, "SS-21 Scarab: Russia's Forgotten (But Deadly) Ballistic Missile," *National Interest*, September 12, 2016b.

Ruane, Kevin, "Refusing to Pay the Price: British Foreign Policy and the Pursuit of Victory in Vietnam, 1952–1954," *The English Historical Review*, Vol. 110, No. 435, February 1995, pp. 70–92.

Rupert, James, "Thousands of Russian Troops in Airport Push," *Newsweek*, January 23, 2015.

Sadowski, David, and Jeff Becker, "Beyond the 'Hybrid' Threat: Asserting the Essential Unity of Warfare," *Small Wars Journal*, 2010.

Salehyan, Idean, "Transnational Rebels: Neighboring States as Sanctuary for Rebel Groups," *World Politics*, Vol. 59, No. 2, 2007, pp. 217–242.

Salmoni, Barak, Bryce Loidolt, and Madeleine Wells, *Regime and Periphery in Northern Yemen: The Huthi Phenomenon*, Santa Monica, Calif.: RAND Corporation, MG-962-DIA, 2010. As of November 9, 2022: https://www.rand.org/pubs/monographs/MG962.html

"Saudi-Led Airstrikes Kill 15 at Wedding in Yemen, Witnesses Say," *Wall Street Journal*, October 7, 2015.

"Saudi-Led Strikes Drive Houthis from Aden," *Al Jazeera*, April 3, 2015.

"Saudi Naval Forces Clear Houthi Mines from Hodeida Coast," *Al Arabiya English*, March 26, 2017.

Schultz, Tammy S., "Tool of Peace and War: Save the Peacekeeping and Stability Operations Institute," Council on Foreign Relations, July 31, 2018.

Shaker, Naseh, "Will Marib Province Survive Houthi Offensive After Fall of al-Jawf?" *Al Monitor*, March 13, 2020.

Shandra, Alya, and Robert Seely, "The Surkov Leaks: The Inner Workings of Russia's Hybrid War in Ukraine," *RUSI Occasional Paper,* July 2019.

Sheldon, Michael, "Russian GPS-Jamming Systems Return to Ukraine," Atlantic Council's Digital Forensic Research Lab, May 23, 2019.

Shen Zhihua, and Xia Yafeng, "Leadership Transfer in the Asian Revolution: Mao Zedong and the Asian Cominform," *Cold War History*, Vol. 14, No. 2, 2014, pp. 195–213.

Shrader, Charles R., *A War of Logistics: Parachutes and Porters in Indochina, 1945–1954*, Lexington, Ky.: University of Kentucky Press, 2015.

Shramovych, Viacheslav, "Ukraine's Deadliest Day: The Battle of Ilovaisk, August 2014," BBC Ukrainian, August 29, 2019.

Shynkareno, Oleg, "Who's Funding East Ukraine Militancy?" Institute for War and Peace, May 16, 2014.

Snow, Shawn, "US MQ-9 Drone Shot Down in Yemen," *Defense News*, October 2, 2017.

Sorley, Lewis, *A Better War: The Unexamined Victories and Final Tragedy of America's Last Years in Vietnam*, New York: Houghton Mifflin Harcourt Publishing, 1999.

South, Todd, "The Army Is Shutting Down Its Highly Praised Asymmetric Warfare Group," *Army Times*, October 2, 2020. As of October 16, 2020: https://www.armytimes.com/news/your-army/2020/10/02/the-army-is-shutting-down-its-much-lauded-asymmetric-warfare-group

"Special Advisory: Naval Mines and MBIEDs off Yemen," *NYA International*, May 19, 2017.

Spector, Ronald H., *After Tet*, New York: The Free Press, 1993.

Stewart, Phil, "U.S. Halting Refueling of Saudi-Led Coalition Aircraft in Yemen's War," Reuters, November 9, 2018.

Stewart, Phil, "U.S. Military Strikes Yemen after Missile Attacks on U.S. Navy Ship," Reuters, October 12, 2016.

Stewart, Phil, "U.S. Navy Ship Targeted in Failed Missile Attack from Yemen: U.S.," Reuters, October 9, 2016.

Stocker, Joanne, "US to Deploy Additional Troops, Patriot Batteries and THAAD System to Saudi Arabia," *The Defense Post*, October 11, 2019.

"Suicide Drones: Houthi Strategic Weapon," Abaad Studies and Research Center, January 2019.

Sukhankin, Sergey, "Russian Electronic Warfare in Ukraine: Between Real and Imaginable," *Eurasian Daily Monitor*, The Jamestown Foundation, May 26, 2017.

Sukhankin, Sergey, "Unleashing the PMCs and Irregulars in Ukraine: Crimea and Donbas," Jamestown Foundation, September 3, 2019.

Summers, Harry G., *On Strategy*, New York: Presidio Press, 1995..

Suslov, Mikhail, "The Production of 'Novorossiya': A Territorial Brand in Public Debates," *Europe-Asia Studies*, Vol. 69, No. 2, 2017.

Sutton, H. I., "Disguised Explosive Boat May Be New Threat to Tankers off Yemen," *Forbes*, March 4, 2020.

Tabatabai, Ariane M., Jeffrey Martini, and Becca Wasser, *The Iran Threat Network (ITN): Four Models of Iran's Nonstate Client Partnerships*, Santa Monica, Calif.: RAND Corporation, RR-4231-A, 2021. As of January 23, 2023: https://www.rand.org/pubs/research_reports/RR4231.html

Taleblu, Behnam Ben, "Analysis: An Iranian SAM in the Arabian Peninsula," *Long War Journal*, April 2, 2018.

Tanham, George Kilpatrick, *Communist Revolutionary Warfare: From the Vietminh to the Viet Cong*, Westport, Conn.: Praeger Security International, 2006.

Throndson, Les, "Combat Survivability with Advanced Aircraft Propulsion Development," *Journal of Aircraft*, Vol. 19, No. 11, November 1982.

Toft, Monica Duffy, and Yuri M. Zhukov, "Denial and Punishment in the North Caucasus: Evaluating the Effectiveness of Coercive Counterinsurgency," *Journal of Peace Research*, Vol. 49, No. 6, 2012, pp. 785–800.

Treisman, Daniel, "Why Putin Took Crimea: The Gambler in the Kremlin," *Foreign Affairs*, May–June 2016.

Trevithick, Joseph, "This Tank Has Become an Icon of Russia's Secret War in Ukraine," *War Is Boring*, June 7, 2016.

Trevithick, Joseph, "Russian GPS-Jamming Systems Return to Ukraine," *The Medium*, May 23, 2019a.

Trevithick, Joseph, "Ukrainian Officer Details Russian Electronic Warfare Tactics Including Radio 'Virus,'" *The Drive*, October 30, 2019b.

Tscetkova, Maria, and Aleksandar Vasovic, "Exclusive: Charred Tanks in Ukraine Point to Russian Involvement," Reuters, October 23, 2014.

United Nations Panel of Experts on Yemen, "Letter to the President of the Security Council," S/2020/70, January 27, 2020.

U.S. Department of Defense, *Summary of the National Defense Strategy of the United States of America: Sharpening the American Military's Competitive Edge*, Washington, D.C., 2018.

U.S. Department of Defense, "Summary of the Irregular Warfare Annex to the National Defense Strategy," 2020.

U.S. Training and Doctrine Command, *Hybrid Threat*, TRADOC TC 7-100, 2010.

U.S. Training and Doctrine Command, *The U.S. Army in Multi-Domain Operations 2028*, TRADOC Pamphlet 525-3-1, December 6, 2018.

U.S. Training and Doctrine Command, *The Operational Environment and the Changing Character of Warfare*, TRADOC Pamphlet 525-92, October 7, 2019.

Valentino, Benjamin A., *Final Solutions: Mass Killing and Genocide in the 20th Century*, Ithaca, N.Y.: Cornell University Press, 2004.

Valentino, Benjamin, Paul Huth, and Dylan Balch-Lindsay, "'Draining the Sea': Mass Killing and Guerrilla Warfare," *International Organization*, Vol. 58, No. 2, Spring 2004, pp. 375–407.

Vandiver, John, "Pentagon to Send More Arms and Equipment to Ukraine," *Stars and Stripes*, June 19, 2019.

Vaughan, Jeremy, Michael Eisenstadt, and Michael Knights, "Missile Attacks on the USS Mason: Principles to Guide U.S. Response," The Washington Institute, October 12, 2016.

Votel, Joseph L., "Terrorism and Iran: Defense Challenges in the Middle East," statement before the House Armed Services Committee on the Posture of U.S. Central Command, February 27, 2018.

Vrolyk, John, "Insurgency, Not War, Is China's Most Likely Course of Action," *War on the Rocks*, December 19, 2019.

Walsh, Declan, and David Kirkpatrick, "U.A.E. Pulls Most Forces from Yemen in Blow to Saudi War Effort," *New York Times*, July 11, 2019.

"WATCH: Yemeni Army Detonates Six Mines Planted by Houthis in Red Sea," *Al Arabiya English*, August 25, 2018.

Waters, Nick, "Houthis Use Armed Drone to Target Yemeni Army Top Brass," *Bellingcat*, January 10, 2019.

Watts, Stephen, J. Michael Polich, and Derek Eaton, "Rapid Regeneration of Irregular Warfare Capacity," *Joint Force Quarterly*, No. 78, 3rd Quarter 2015, pp. 32–39.

Watts, Stephen, Patrick B. Johnston, Jennifer Kavanagh, Sean M. Zeigler, Bryan Frederick, Trevor Johnston, Karl P. Mueller, Astrid Stuth Cevallos, Nathan Chandler, Meagan L. Smith, Alexander Stephenson, and Julia A. Thompson, *Limited Intervention: Evaluating the Effectiveness of Limited Stabilization, Limited Strike, and Containment Operations*, Santa Monica, Calif.: RAND Corporation, RR-2037-A, 2017. As of November 1, 2022: https://www.rand.org/pubs/research_reports/RR2037.html

Weiss, Caleb, "Analysis: Houthi Drone Strikes in Saudi Arabia and Yemen," *Long War Journal*, August 7, 2019.

Weiss, Caleb, "Analysis: Houthi Naval Attacks in the Red Sea," *Long War Journal*, August 17, 2019.

Weiss, Caleb, "Houthis Kill Over 100 Yemeni Soldiers in Missile, Drone Attack on Base," *Long War Journal*, January 20, 2020.

White House, *National Security Strategy of the United States of America*, Washington, D.C., December 2017.

Wiest, Andrew, and Chris McNab, *The Vietnam War*, New York: Cavendish Square Publishing, 2016.

Winter, Lucas, "The Adaptive Transformation of Yemen's Republican Guard," *Small Wars Journal*, March 2017.

El Yaakoubi, Aziz, "Saudi-Led Coalition Air Strikes in Yemen Down 80%: U.N. Envoy," Reuters, November 22, 2019.

"Yemen Conflict: US Strikes Radar Sites After Missile Attack on Ship," BBC News, October 13, 2016.

"Yemen: Houthi Landmines Kill Civilians, Block Aid," Human Rights Watch, April 22, 2019.

"Yemen: Houthis Claim Attack on UAE Military Vessel," *Al Jazeera*, October 2, 2016.

Yemen Polling Center, "Perceptions of the Yemeni Public on Security-Related Issues: Survey Findings, Sanaa/Aden," August 2019. As of November 14, 2022: https://yemenpolling.org/Projects-en/ICSP_Survey_2019_Preliminary_findings_26_01_2020.pdf

"Yemen Soldiers Killed in Houthi Drone Attack on Base," BBC News, January 10, 2019.

"Yemen War: US Ship Faces New Round of 'Houthi Missiles'," *Al Jazeera*, October 16, 2016.

Zasloff, Joseph Jermiah, *The Role of the Sanctuary in Insurgency: Communist China's Support to the Vietminh*, 1946-1954, RAND Corporation, RM-4618-PR, 1967. As of November 2, 2022:
https://www.rand.org/pubs/research_memoranda/RM4618.html